Duddin[g]

its story in 50 objects

Edited by Jacquetta Megarry on behalf of Duddingston Conservation Society

Duddingston: its story in 50 objects

First published in 2019 on behalf of Duddingston Conservation Society
(see page 93) by
Rucksack Readers
6 Old Church Lane
Edinburgh
EH15 3PX, UK

Telephone   0131 661 0262
Website   *www.rucsacs.com*

The maps in this book were produced from Open StreetMap:
openstreetmap.org with additional material from field surveys by the
editor.

British Library cataloguing in publication data: a catalogue record for
this book is available from the British Library.

ISBN 978-1-898481-88-1

Designed in Scotland by Ian Clydesdale (*www.workhorse.scot*)

Printed in the UK by Blackmore Ltd on responsibly sourced paper

Readers are responsible for their own welfare and safety. All
information has been checked carefully prior to publication, but
information such as opening hours is liable to change. If you
encounter any problems or have any updates, please email your
comments to *jacquetta@rucsacs.com*.

Updates will be posted on the web page *www.rucsacs.com/books/dcs*.

Contents

Preface   4

Introduction   6

Duddingston's place in Scotland's story   8

Reverend John Thomson   12

1 Duddingston Kirk   15

2 Norman arches   20

3 Stained glass   22

4 Gatehouse   24

5 Graveyard entrance   26

6 Graveyard   27

7 Manse and garden   30

8 Garden Room & Millar Hall   32

9 The glebe   33

10 Dr Neils Garden   34

11 The Telford Bridge   36

12 The Physic Garden   37

13 The Thomson Tower   38

14 Duddingston Loch   40

15 Bawsinch Nature Reserve   42

16 Reedbeds and Duddingston Hardings 43

17 Holyrood Park   44

18 Arthur's Seat   46

19 Dunsapie Crag and Loch   48

20 Duddingston Hoard   49

21 Miniature coffins   50

22 Park entrance   51

23 The Sheep Heid   52

24 The snuff box   54

25 Skittles alley   55

26 Sheep Heid memorabilia   56

27 Old Church Lane   58

28 Wall plaque   61

29 12 Old Church Lane   62

30 The Home House   63

31 The Causeway   64

32 Bonnie Prince Charlie house   68

33 Charlescote and its wall   69

34 Hawthorn Brae   70

35 Lochside Cottage   71

36 Community Land   72

37 The field   74

38 The byre   76

39 Vegetable garden   77

40 Duddingston House   78

41 Courtyard   82

42 The pleasure gardens   83

43 The temple   84

44 Duddingston Golf Club   85

45 War memorials   86

46 Lady Nairne's Lodge   87

47 Cauvin's Hospital   88

48 Duddingston crossroads   89

49 Prestonfield House   90

50 The Innocent railway   92

Practical information   93

Glossary   94

Further reading and credits   95

Index   96

Preface

This is the story of Duddingston, told through people who lived long ago and by those who live today; of buildings, a volcano, gardens, lochs, a golf course, a pub, a kirk, a railway, a minister's love affair, parties long ago and aristocrats and kings – a unique mix, and a microcosm of human society.

Edinburgh contains a number of villages, but Duddingston stands out. It has spectacular geographical features, and Holyrood Park separates it from the centre of Edinburgh – but surprisingly it has no guidebook. As Chairman of Duddingston Conservation Society, I wanted us to produce a book about our area to celebrate our 60th anniversary. Back in 1975 we had helped our neighbourhood to achieve Conservation Area status: the map opposite shows its extent as extended in 2007 to include the entire Innocent cycleway and footpath.

Telling our story through objects was inspired by Neil MacGregor's book and broadcasts *A History of the World in 100 Objects*. Duddingston has been occupied for a few thousand years, and we have told our stories mainly from a human angle. The area has attracted more than its fair share of characters, eccentrics and a few buffoons.

Duddingston has a strong sense of community, and our members have been involved in this book, both in selecting the objects and in documenting their stories. Our objects are extremely diverse: you will find things ranging in antiquity from the Bronze Age Hoard to the 21st century vegetable garden on our Community Land. Objects vary in size from a famous snuff box to the broad expanse of 650-acre Holyrood Park. Welcome to the story of Duddingston in 50 objects.

Malcolm Windsor, Chairman,
Duddingston Conservation Society
October 2019

Introduction

This book is for anybody who is interested in Duddingston – residents, daytrippers who stumble upon the village by accident, and holidaymakers from afar who plan for their time in the capital to include its best-kept secret.

It is a remarkable place: within a small area stand several outstanding Grade-A Listed Buildings*, notably Duddingston Kirk and Duddingston House, dating respectively from the early 12th and mid-18th centuries. It claims Scotland's oldest pub, the Sheep Heid, and Edinburgh's oldest railway, the Innocent. Visitors can wander around the plants and trees of secluded Dr Neils Garden, enjoy wildlife in the nature reserve of Duddingston Loch or take a meal in the attractive surroundings of Duddingston Golf Club. They can even climb Arthur's Seat, the extinct volcano in Holyrood Park that provides Edinburgh's highest viewpoint: see pages 46-7.

In telling Duddingston's story we chose our objects carefully, and struggled to keep the number down to 50. All can be seen and enjoyed by any visitor, albeit in some cases you need to check opening hours before setting out. Also, some objects are private homes and although you can see these houses from the pavement, please respect the residents' privacy. And Object 43 is in the middle of a golf course so you cannot safely or responsibly approach it unless certain that no golf is in play.

North-west over Duddingston village

We focus mainly on objects inside the official Conservation Area, with a handful just outside. Only two Objects (20 and 21) are a couple of miles from Duddingston, on display in the National Museum of Scotland: see page 95. We didn't feel constrained by slavish rules: our criterion for inclusion was whether the object tells an interesting story and has relevant images. Most stand alone, but in a few cases a couple of objects are juxtaposed on a single page. Eight are important enough to justify the inclusion of associated objects – either inside them or nearby.

All the main locations are identified on the map inside our back cover. We have included practical information about getting here, with opening times and refreshment options: see page 93.

We want to encourage readers to explore Duddingston on foot, and when visiting these objects to reflect on their stories, many of them strange and remarkable. Collecting and illustrating them has led us to notice details, to investigate puzzles and to keep our eyes wide open.

We begin with an essay that establishes Duddingston's place in Scotland's story, then introduce its famous painting minister, John Thomson, whose name crops up throughout the book. The 50 Objects then follow in what we intend as a logical sequence, but some people may prefer to dip in at random. For readers unfamiliar with architectural or religious terminology, and for those who may struggle with Scottish vernacular, we provide a Glossary as well as an index.

* See Listed Buildings entry on page 94.

Duddingston's place in Scotland's story

Landscapes bear witness to events that took place millions of years ago. This is strikingly clear in Duddingston. The small volcano now known as Arthur's Seat has not erupted for over 320 million years, yet it still dominates the village in its shadow, and its volcanic soils dictate what flourishes in our gardens today.

James Hutton

James Hutton (1726-97) was the founder of modern geology and did much of his work around Arthur's Seat. Indeed part of Salisbury Crags is still known as Hutton's section. His ideas provided the very long timescale that enabled Darwin to make natural selection credible in his theory of evolution of species.

At the end of the last Ice Age, erosion by a retreating glacier exposed the Salisbury Crags and scooped out Duddingston Loch. Material that the glacier left behind prevented the marshy area to the west from draining. Much of the character of the Bawsinch Nature Reserve is a legacy of this glacial activity.

The oldest evidence of human habitation in the Edinburgh area is from Cramond, and dates back to about 8500 BC. These people would have been hunter-gatherers. It is not known whether Duddingston was settled at around this time, but people had certainly arrived by the Bronze Age (c. 2500-700 BC). The Duddingston Hoard (see page 49) dates to between 1000 and 750 BC. By this time agricultural techniques had arrived in Scotland and it seems likely that these early settlers were responsible for some of the cultivation terraces on Crow Hill and Arthur's Seat: see pages 44-5.

These people left few traces of their existence or way of life. It was from the early 12th century AD that recorded events began to shape the village of Duddingston as we know it today. The founding of Duddingston Kirk in 1124 established the heart of a community in this area.

Christianity had come to southern Scotland during the Roman occupation of much of Britain. However, as Roman influence declined, Christianity largely disappeared. From the 6th century, it was reintroduced by missionaries, many of them Irish. From the 8th century the Celtic church they had established gradually began to give way to Roman Catholicism.

1124
Duddingston Kirk begun

1100

1200

1070-93
Queen Margaret

1124-1153
King David 1

1250
Queen Margaret
made a saint

8

The church in Scotland remained only loosely organised until well into the 11th century. In the later part of that century, however, significant change began under the influence of Queen Margaret. Margaret was a Saxon princess who fled from England after the Norman conquest in 1066, and by 1070 had married Malcolm III of Scotland.

Margaret and Malcolm

Her strong influence extended after her death in 1093 through three of her sons who reigned in succession. In the period up to 1153, extensive reform of the church in Scotland resulted in the founding of many abbeys and the establishment of a system of bishoprics and parishes. Margaret was proclaimed a saint in 1250 by Pope Innocent IV.

The building of the church at Duddingston was thus part of an organised programme of church reform. King David I, who reigned between 1124 and 1153, was very active in encouraging the building of abbeys.

Indeed Duddingston Kirk was built on land that he granted to the abbey at Kelso. The Kirk was the place of worship for an extensive parish that included not only Duddingston but also Portobello, Joppa and much of what today is eastern Edinburgh.

In medieval times, there was little development near the coast. What is now known as Duddingston village was generally referred to as Wester Duddingston. The main street was the Causeway which continued westwards down the Vennel to the loch, with a branch that led to the Kirk. The thoroughfare now known as Old Church Lane did not exist, although there were cottages occupying at least part of the land where the current 19th century houses stand. Some people were undoubtedly involved in agriculture; others worked in a variety of trades including weaving.

Throughout the middle ages there was one universal church in western Europe. However, in 1517 Martin Luther nailed his 95 Theses (arguments against church practices) to a church door in Wittenberg, Germany, thus launching the Reformation. Over the following 20 years many German states and countries in northern Europe converted to some form of Protestantism. Meanwhile Scotland remained faithful to Roman Catholicism, but in 1560 it became the last country wholly to break away from the Catholic Church.

The effect on Kirk worship is described on page 17. In many respects the reformed church was repressive and

1360
Sheep Heid established

1631
Kirk North Aisle completed

1300

1600

1560
Scottish
Reformation

1567–1625 James VI/I
1582
Edinburgh University founded

9

authoritarian, using primitive forms of humiliation such as the jougs: see page 26. However, Protestantism also helped to create a new and more questioning intellectual climate.

The 18th century saw dramatic change in Scotland. It began with economic crisis caused by the collapse of the Darien

The 8th Earl of Abercorn

Scheme. A disputed succession to the throne would lead to the two significant Jacobite uprisings, and the controversial parliamentary Union with England divided opinion deeply. Bonnie Prince Charlie, leader of the second Jacobite uprising, made his battle plans for Prestonpans in Duddingston in 1745: see page 57.

By this time the village had around 500 inhabitants, many living in primitive thatched cottages. Only 15 years after 1745, the 8th Earl of Abercorn would commission Duddingston House, less

than a mile away: see page 78. He had no need to fortify it against possible warfare on his doorstep.

By the late 18th century, the Jacobite threat had receded and Scotland had become more prosperous. Its citizens largely supported both the Union and the Hanoverian succession – celebrated in street names in Edinburgh's New Town. The Earl of Abercorn aimed to transform Wester Duddingston village into a modern middle-class enclave suited to people who wanted a country retreat. The hill and loch provided a pleasant rural backdrop, and in winter the frozen loch encouraged sports such as curling and skating. After the Duddingston Curling Society was formed in 1795, its rules were quickly adopted by other clubs: see page 39. During the 19th century, Britain led the world in organised sport, and defined the rules for many other sports.

The questioning intellectual ethos that began to emerge after the Reformation eventually gave rise to the Scottish Enlightenment. This refers to a period between about 1730 and 1820 when various Scottish thinkers made an extraordinary contribution to the modern world. The movement is associated with scepticism and empiricism, and its advocates rejected ideas that could not be justified by reason. Whilst its leading figures were primarily philosophers, the Scottish Enlightenment also had a strong practical dimension. Engineers such as James Watt made Scotland a pioneer of the Industrial Revolution.

	1745 Battle of Prestonpans	1760–1769 Duddingston House built	1795 Curling Society founded	1805–1840 John Thomson's ministry
1700			**1800**	
1707 Act of Union	1715 1st Jacobite rebellion	1745 2nd Jacobite rebellion	1783 RSE established	1815 Waterloo / 1822 George IV visits Edinburgh

The new interest in science and medicine had an unintended and macabre impact on Duddingston. Edinburgh University's medical school began teaching anatomy, thus creating a demand for bodies for dissection. This led to a lucrative business for grave robbers: see page 24.

Nowhere is more closely associated with the Enlightenment than Edinburgh. All the leading figures lived in Edinburgh for at least part of their lives, and the role of its clubs and coffee houses was crucial. Duddingston was close to the centre of Enlightenment thinking and hosted many of its key figures.

A notable example was John Thomson, minister at the Kirk from 1805-1840: see pages 12-14. His contribution to the intellectual and artistic life of his times was important, and he brought many distinguished visitors to the village – including Walter Scott, who pioneered the historical novel, and J M W Turner, arguably Britain's greatest painter.

The appearance of Duddingston Village today is marked by 19th century development. Nearly all of Old Church Lane dates from this period, as does the western end of the Causeway. The rebuilding of the Sheep Heid dates from the 1850s: see page 52.

Duddingston, like the country as a whole, was affected by major events of the 20th century. The slaughter of World War 1 took its toll here, with a long list of names on the war memorials. The fate of the Hay family who lost three sons is recorded in the Kirk's stained glass: see page 22.

During the 20th century the remaining gaps in the development were filled in. Two prime sites near the loch were developed in the first two decades. In 1962-3 modern homes were built around the north-east corner of the Causeway. A row of new houses was built on the former drying green during the 1970s, with a final house added about 1999. As part of plans to renovate Duddingston House and its courtyard, new houses were built there during 1990/91.

Over the years Duddingston has remained distinct from the city of which it is now part. In this book, we tell Duddingston's story in the context of the part it has played in wider events.

* The Society for the Preservation of Duddingston Village (SPDV) changed its name twice and is now Duddingston Conservation Society (DCS)

| Development of Duddingston Village | 1959 Formation of SPDV* | 1979 McNiven Bequest | 1990 Courtyard Houses | 2014 DCS* buys Community Land |

1900   **2000**

| 1837–1901 Queen Victoria | 1914–1918 World War 1 | 1939–1945 World War 2 |

Reverend John Thomson
(1778-1840)

A conscientious minister of the Church of Scotland by profession, John Thomson was just as serious about his art as his ministry. He was a passionate amateur painter, largely self-taught. His landscapes received wide approval and created high demand, but he never pursued commercial success or fame. He painted out of his love of Scotland's scenery and his compulsion to portray it. He would spend hours 'striving to make an exact portrait of a graceful or majestic tree or rock – to catch the exact effect of ... sparkling water trickling below foliage in a stray sunbeam'.

Portrait of Thomson by Henry Raeburn

Just as his friend Walter Scott was much more than a Clerk of Session, John Thomson was much more than a minister. He was a major player in the development of the Scottish school of landscape painting. In parallel with Scott awakening interest in the Highlands with his novels and poetry, Thomson was celebrating its magnificent scenery in his watercolours and oil paintings. He travelled widely, sketchbook in hand, and worked tirelessly at capturing the moods and light in Scottish landscapes.

Before Thomson, landscape painting was largely of romantic scenes from Italy, Holland or England, not Scotland. Wealthy Scottish families were more likely to have portraits on their walls than landscapes, and most houses had no paintings of any kind. In the early 19th century, Edinburgh had no formal bodies for the arts and opportunities for artists to exhibit were scarce. Over the next two decades, all that changed.

Thomson's life began in 1778, when he was born in the manse at Dailly, Ayrshire, the fourth son of the parish minister Thomas Thomson. The youngest of eight children, he was educated at Dailly Parish School. He seems to have been inspired by the Ayrshire countryside and showed both talent and commitment to landscape painting from an early age.

In 1791 (aged 13) he enrolled at Glasgow University to study law and theology, but two years later transferred to Edinburgh University to study divinity. While there, he met many people who were prominent in Edinburgh artistic circles, including Alexander Nasmyth, who gave him art lessons for a month, and Walter Scott, who became a lifelong friend.

After graduating, Thomson returned to Ayrshire and was licensed as a minister in 1799. The next year he was offered the living as minister at Dailly, thus following in his father's footsteps. In 1801 he married Isabella Ramsay who died in 1809. They had five children, of whom one died in infancy. In 1805 he was offered the ministry at Duddingston, where he remained until his death in 1840.

He remarried in 1813 to a widow, Frances Ingram Spence, who was also an accomplished artist. They had a further five children together, of whom one died in infancy. In addition to these eight surviving children whom Thomson had fathered, the manse was home to three of Frances' children from her marriage to Marten Dalrymple.

Some assume that the moniker 'a' Jock Tamson's bairns' refers to this 11-child household. More probably it came from his affectionate habit of calling his parishioners, 'ma' bairns' (my children) – to which they would respond 'We're a' Jock Tamson's bairns'.

In 1814 he was elected a Fellow of the Royal Society of Edinburgh: his proposers included John Playfair and Sir David Brewster. Playfair was a polymath, a minister, scientist and mathematician who was best known for his summary of the work of James Hutton, the father of modern geology. Sir David Brewster was a friend and Principal of Edinburgh University. The RSE was a hive of Enlightenment activity and its Fellows embraced a wide range of interests. Thomson published articles on physical science in the Edinburgh Review.

Thomson's studio beside the loch

John Thomson's artistic reputation soon grew, and many visitors came to his studio in the Thomson Tower on the edge of Duddingston Loch: see page 38. During J M W Turner's visit in 1818, the famous artist commented 'By God sir, I envy you that piece of water'. Thomson and Turner both produced paintings of rural Scottish features and scenes to illustrate a book entitled *The Provincial Antiquities of Scotland*, with text by Walter Scott. Baird (Thomson's biographer, whose partiality is very obvious) clearly preferred Thomson's paintings.

By this time Thomson's oil paintings had been exhibited regularly, notably in Henry Raeburn's gallery in York Place. In 1819, the Royal Institution for the Encouragement of the Fine Arts was established, and Thomson was elected as an Honorary Member. More exhibitions followed, and in 1826 the Royal Scottish Academy was formed and Thomson became an Honorary Fellow. He was invited to contribute paintings to its annual exhibitions from 1831 to 1840.

In his Duddingston years, Thomson was a family man, a minister and also a sociable host. The manse was the scene of much entertaining and Thomson was not only affable but also a good listener. He was an excellent friend to Walter Scott and they frequently travelled together into the Highlands. Scott was seven years older than Thomson, but they admired each other's work and were both passionate about nature and art.

Thomson's excellent grasp of landscape detail helped Scott with descriptions in his novels.

When Scott died after contracting typhus in 1832, aged only 61, Thomson was greatly affected. Their friendship had been long-standing and very warm. Scott had been a frequent visitor at the manse and Thomson had visited Abbotsford many times. Thomson later travelled with another good friend, Sir David Brewster, who succeeded to an estate near Aviemore. This led to a number of grand paintings in and around Strathspey.

Until early 1840 Thomson had enjoyed very good health, but he declined abruptly during the year and became unable to take outdoor exercise. He struggled on with sermons and art through the summer, but he made his last painting in September 1840.

By 27 October he had declined so far that he had his bed moved to the window to enjoy that glorious view for the last time. By the next morning, he had died at the early age of 62. His second wife, Frances, survived him until 1845.

Thomson had spent 35 of his 41 years of ministry at Duddingston. Later he was given an elaborate tomb in the north-west corner of the Kirkyard, which also commemorates his two wives and daughter Margaret. The top of the tomb bears a lengthy Latin inscription which refers to his exceptional gifts, the gentleness and purity of his disposition and his extreme benevolence.

In 1903 his nephew, Lockhart Thomson, commissioned the memorial stained glass window that stands inside the Kirk just west of the pulpit: see page 17.

The Thomson tomb, north-west graveyard

1 Duddingston Kirk

The kirk has stood for 900 years. It takes pride of place as the most historically important and architecturally distinguished building in Duddingston, and it is our first Object.

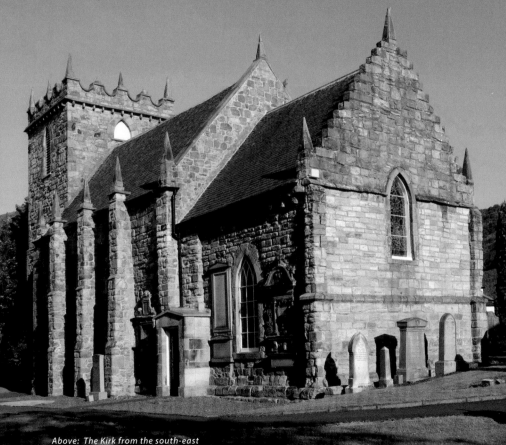

Above: The Kirk from the south-east
Top: The burning bush, emblem of the Church of Scotland since 1691

The earliest parts of the Kirk date back to 1124, the year in which King David 1, the youngest of Queen Margaret's sons (see page 9), came to the throne of Scotland. It is thus one of Edinburgh's oldest buildings, probably older than St Margaret's Chapel in Edinburgh Castle, and one of a very small group of local churches such as Dalmeny and Kirkliston that were founded in the 12th century. The building was commissioned by Dodin, a Norman knight who gave his name to Dodinstoun or Duddingston. It was built on land that had been granted to Kelso Abbey, which retained its ownership until the Reformation.

The original building was small and quite plain. It did not extend as far west as the present tower and did not include the large aisle

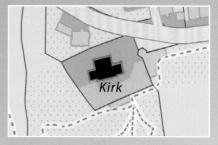

to the north where the main body of seating is now situated. The church was orientated on an east-west axis and entry was by a door on the south side.

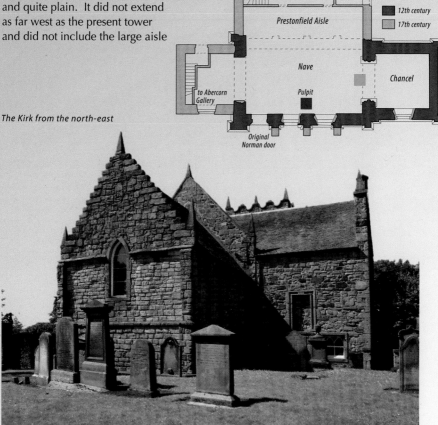

The Kirk from the north-east

Like almost all early churches, it had an altar situated at the east end where the priest said Mass. The congregation would have stood or sat in the western arm. Two fine Norman arches survive from this early period and are still clearly visible – one, on the outside of the south wall, with unique and enigmatic sculptures, and the other dividing the chancel from the remainder of the church: see page 20.

The church remained little altered until after the Reformation. In 1560, with surprisingly little bloodshed, Scotland adopted a Calvinist version of Protestantism known as Presbyterianism. Duddingston Kirk, like the great majority of Scottish churches, became a Protestant place of worship. The new kind of services brought about changes in the way the building was used and, over time, in its very structure.

Protestantism had less need of ceremonial and, therefore, less use for the short processional route eastwards

towards the altar. Instead, the focus was on the preaching of the Word. It became important that the whole congregation should be able to hear – and, ideally, also see – the minister. This determined the nature of the modifications that would be made to the building.

In 1631 the Prestonfield Aisle was added to the north of the original body of the church, almost doubling its size, with a large balcony above.

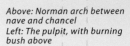

Above: Norman arch between nave and chancel
Left: The pulpit, with burning bush above

Today the Aisle accommodates the bulk of the seating. The entire orientation of the church changed, so that its axis became north/south. The congregation faces towards the minister and the pulpit is in the middle of the nave of the original structure. In effect, it has become a preaching hall, in exact accord with Presbyterian requirements.

The chancel had been the focus of worship, and was where at least one local landowner was buried. A tablet on the north wall of the chancel (dated 10 January 1603) commemorates the laird, Alexander Thomson, and his wife, Margaret Preston. It bears their coat of arms and initials, with an inscription *Dies mortis aeternae vitae natalis est fidelibus* or 'On the day that they die the faithful are born into eternal life'.

The chancel also contains a recess into the stone of the wall. One theory about its purpose holds that it was a 'leper squint' or window through which lepers could observe the service without putting the congregation at risk. A more likely theory is that it was an *aumbry* or cupboard where sacred vessels and consecrated bread and wine could be stored for use during the Mass. If so, then this small niche is a surviving relic of Catholic practice in a building otherwise adapted for Presbyterian worship.

Upper: Memorial tablet, 1603
Lower: Chancel north wall with aumbry ✓
Facing page: The 17th century tower

After the Prestonfield Aisle was built, the chancel became almost peripheral. For a while it was the location of the 'Laird's loft', a balcony for the exclusive use of the local landowner and his family. In 1889 a pipe organ was installed in its place but this later fell into disrepair and was removed, thus opening up the view into the chancel much as it would have been in the 12th century.

The most conspicuous addition to the exterior was in the later 17th century, when the church was extended westward and a bell-tower erected. The square tower is not very tall but looks imposing, with its eight pinnacles and gothic-style windows. A gallery with seating, known as the Abercorn Gallery, was installed immediately under the tower in 1825. The Kirk's structure has not been significantly changed since, but there has been much restoration. Renovations were undertaken in 1825, 1865 and in 1889 by the well-known Edinburgh architect Robert Rowand Anderson. Further work was undertaken in 1968.

The influence of large landowners was the issue over which the church split in 1843. At the Disruption, a third of the ministers left the official church to found the Free Church of Scotland. Although Duddingston Kirk remained loyal to the official church, sectarian differences affected its relationship with parts of its parish.

The parish extended far beyond the village and took in the developing suburb of Portobello and the seaside area of Joppa. A subordinate church or Chapel of Ease was set up in Portobello in 1818, but parishioners still had to travel to Duddingston for any important events such as burials. The church in Portobello remained subordinate to the Kirk Session in Duddingston. After a while, tensions in the community led to the division of the original parish in 1834.

Over the years the parish has attracted many dedicated ministers, the best known of whom was the Rev John Thomson: see pages 12-14. Many remained in post over long periods: remarkably the present minister, the Rev Dr Jim Jack, is only the 21st incumbent since the Reformation.

Duddingston Kirk has evolved over the last 900 years, and its present structure would be unrecognisable to a villager returning from the early 12th century. Yet much of the original stonework of the east and south walls and probably also some of the roof timbers remain. Scotland has few medieval churches: Duddingston is fortunate to have one of the most beautiful and interesting.

2 Norman arches

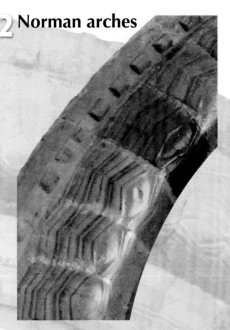

There are two 12th century Norman arches – this page features the large interior arch. Originally it fulfilled the important function of separating the nave (where the congregation stood or sat) from the chancel containing the altar (where the priest celebrated mass, largely hidden from view).

The arch is unusually large and well-preserved. It is over ten feet wide, and features geometric chevrons and notches, with scalloped capitals on the columns.

A smaller arch framed the former main doorway outside to the south. It was blocked up in the 17th century when the Prestonfield Aisle created the chance to make a door on the sheltered opposite side of the building.

Top: Chevrons on the chancel arch
Below: East towards the chancel

Many Norman arches are found throughout Scotland, but the Duddingston doorway is unique in having sculptures carved into its left column.

On the upper left column is the gowned figure of Christ on the cross. Beneath it is the figure of Abraham holding a long dagger aloft, about to sacrifice his son Isaac: see close-up photos below, left and centre. Just to one side is the ram that God provided for the sacrifice. These sculptures reminded medieval worshippers of the Christian message and are symbols of Old and New Testament sacrifice.

Although eroded by centuries of weathering, these sculptures are still discernible – and different from the carved chevrons of the right column and round arch above.

Above: Former main doorway
Below: Details from the former doorway

Stained glass

The Ascension window in the east wall of the former chancel is the modern window shown on the right. It commemorates Bailie John Hay and his wife Jane Mackie 'who laboured for this kirk from 1884-1944'. A subtle feature of this window lies in the four disciples representing the Hay sons: three of their faces are colourless, symbolising the three who died during World War 1. They are shown in the regimental colours that the brothers wore when they served. Two Hay daughters sit above the risen Christ, already in heaven and playing their musical instruments. The Hay brothers also feature in the War Memorial and the 'Dead Men's Pennies': see page 28.

On either side of the pulpit are two windows that, although Victorian in appearance, date from the early 20th century. On the left is the Good Shepherd, a tribute to Dr Stevenson Macadam, an elder of the Kirk and brother of John Macadam, the chemist. A new edible nut was discovered in Brisbane in 1857 and named macadamia after John Macadam by his colleague who was Director of the Royal Botanical Gardens in Australia. On the right, the St Luke window celebrates the Rev John Thomson: it was commissioned by his nephew Lockhart Thomson in his uncle's memory, and erected in 1903.

Above the Prestonfield Aisle is the trio of stained glass windows by Douglas Strachan (1875-1950), a leading Scottish designer of stained glass windows in the 20th century. They depict Works of Mercy and were a gift from the daughter of Joan Carfrae Pinkerton. Frances Ingram Spence (Rev

John Thomson's second wife, see page 13) had given generous and sympathetic help to her mother, Joan Pinkerton, which she celebrated by the gift of these windows. Back in 1842, Joan Pinkerton had married Allan Pinkerton who founded the famous Pinkerton Detective Agency in the US.

Above: Memorial to John Hay and Jane Mackie
Facing page: The Pinkerton memorial window

Except ye be converted and become as little children

Suffer the little children to come unto me for of such is the Kingdom of heaven

4 Gatehouse

In the 18th century, Edinburgh University started to train medical students in dissection instead of sending them off to Holland. Corpses were required for this purpose, but the belief about bodily resurrection was so strong that no one wanted to donate their body for teaching purposes. This gave rise to the Resurrectionists – those who stole freshly buried bodies and sold them to the medical school. People at the school's back door received the bodies, asked no questions and paid £10 to £12 per corpse – the equivalent of an annual salary for a labourer.

By the 1820s, the fear of the body snatchers was great, and in 1824 a gatehouse – a hexagonal tower designed by Robert Brown – was erected at the Kirk entrance. This provided a lookout post to protect new graves for the first three weeks after each burial. The watch was provided by paid help or by a rota among the elders. Fresh corpses commanded the highest price. After three weeks, the corpse was considered not worth stealing, so the watch was no longer needed.

A young woman Annie Stewart (aged 18) was buried late one afternoon in a shallow grave, and her coffin dug up a few hours later by two snatchers, one the notorious John Samuel. They were to pay a high price for their attempted crime.

When they prised open the coffin lid, young Annie was revived by the cold night air and sat up screaming. This apparent resurrection caused extreme terror in the would-be snatchers.

They fled in different directions – one ran to the loch and swam away, never to be caught, but John Samuel went towards the city centre and was captured in a wild and mad condition. He was later tried and hanged. Young Annie was more fortunate: the commotion attracted the attention of the minister and beadle, who carried her to the manse where she was cared for. She went on to make a full recovery, and was later married in the Kirk. After her baby boy was baptised there, the family emigrated to Maxton, North Carolina.

Soon a change in the law required that the bodies of all who died in prison would be given to the medical school, ending the market for corpses. By the 1840s the gatehouse had become a meeting room for the Kirk elders and an office or vestry for the minister.

Grave robbers at work

The gatehouse (1824)

5 Graveyard entrance

As you face the gateway into the graveyard, to the right the jougs (a hinged iron collar) hang from the wall, with the loupin-on stane (literally 'leaping on stone') nearby: see below. At least 11 old parish churches in Scotland still have jougs, but Duddingston is unusual in that it also retains its mounting steps as well as its watchtower. This unique collection shows us clearly how a kirkyard entry would have appeared over 200 years ago.

The loupin-on stane dates from the 17th century and is Grade B-listed in its own right. The four stone steps lead to a platform from which parishioners could easily mount and dismount their horses – while also helping gentlewomen to safeguard their modesty. During services horses were often stabled at the Sheep Heid in the area now occupied by its car park.

Jougs were an instrument of punishment and humiliation. They were sometimes set up at the mercat cross, but more often at the parish church. Two halves of an iron collar were attached to a wall by means of a short chain. An offender's neck was placed in the collar and secured by a padlock. The jougs fulfilled much the same function as wooden stocks, but needed much less space.

In each parish the Kirk Session had the power to inflict punishments for a wide range of offences such as drunkenness, profanity, disrespect of the Sabbath and sexual irregularities. Before the Sunday service culprits had to endure the jougs and afterwards, dressed in sackcloth, they stood at the kirk door. During the service, they had to sit on a Stool of Repentance in front of the congregation.

Often the punishment was repeated over a number of Sundays. In 1660 Susan Douglas and David Howeyson, adulterers, were made to appear at Duddingston no less than 17 times. The same form of punishment was used in the Netherlands by the strictly Calvinist Dutch Reformed Church.

Inset: The jougs. Below: Loupin-on stane

6 Graveyard

The graveyard is a fascinating and tranquil place to explore. There are nearly 120 memorials of various kinds, yet the great majority of graves are now unmarked. The poor were interred in shallow graves marked with simple wooden crosses – none of which survive. The resting places of the rich range from elaborate stone tablets with extensive inscriptions to large vaults guarded by iron gates, padlocks and mortsafes – to protect themselves from the Resurrectionists. Their graves were also much deeper: deep graves cost more to dig, but were safer from grave robbers. The graveyard reminds us of how unequally wealth was shared.

Many of the elaborate tombs bear long inscriptions, some still legible. John Thomson's extensively inscribed tomb is in the north-west corner: see page 14. A more surprising inclusion near the western wall is the ivy-clad arched gravestone for the Rev Mackintosh MacKay. By the time of his death in 1873, he had served as a minister for 48 years. However his burial in Duddingston demonstrates tolerance from the Church of Scotland; while a minister in Dunoon, MacKay had walked

Rev Mackintosh MacKay gravestone

out of the General Assembly to help form the Free Church at the time of the Disruption in 1843. Although the churches were reunited much later (1929), relations were strained during the 19th century.

Strongly protected vaults of the wealthy

had to be paid for each letter engraved, hence the concise six-letter inscription: 'Wee Jim'.

Compare the simplicity of Wee Jim's grave with the ornate and extensive carvings in the memorial on the south wall of the Kirk shown opposite. It is inscribed to David Scot, Margaret Gourley and their eight children. Ionic columns support a curved pediment above, with decorations of elaborate scrolls, statues, a memento mori skull and an angel. The date is given as 'the 20 of Aperil [sic] 1693'.

Opposite the Kirk door are two other interesting graves. Alexander Hay was one of three brothers killed in the Great War. He and his brothers William Mackie and John Douglas Hay are commemorated in the War Memorial inscription beside the Kirk entrance and in a stained glass window inside. Behind it on the graveyard wall there are three round metal discs known as Dead Men's Pennies – struck in a London foundry for every soldier killed in the war.

It is easy to overlook the simplest of all gravestones: deeply shaded under a tree near the west wall stands a Celtic cross bearing the simple inscription 'Wee Jim' – with no date and no surname. The story, passed on for generations through the women of the Kirk, was of a poor young woman who worked in the notorious flax industry at Portobello. Unmarried and having given birth to a son, she would have been shunned by the majority.

Depending on her income for survival, and having nobody else to look after the child, she had no option but to take her young son to work. In that harsh, damp environment, the child caught pneumonia and died. Her fellow workers collected enough money to finance a small gravestone. The stonemason

Above: Wee Jim's grave
Below: The Hay brothers' Pennies

India Company. Haldane had been brought up by his grandfather Patrick, Laird of Gleneagles, to whom the obelisk is dedicated.

Haldane and 48 others died in the sinking of the Nancy off the Scilly Isles in 1784. The small tender boat in the foreground shows a figure of a woman with a baby, a reference to John Haldane's mistress, a 23-year old famous opera singer called Ann Cargill, who drowned in the same shipwreck. Her body was later found ashore, still holding the baby in her arms.

Edinburgh has many splendid graveyards. Some are much larger, such as Greyfriars, with over 700 memorials. Others house more famous people, such as Adam Smith (Canongate) and David Hume (Old Calton). However Duddingston's enjoys a uniquely rural setting in the lee of Arthur's Seat, and its memorials convey a peaceful sense of continuity.

To the left stands an obelisk with an unusual marble relief depicting a shipwreck in stormy seas. This celebrates the life of one John Haldane who by 1779 had become a captain for the East

Above: The Scot/Gourley memorial
Below : Marble relief on the obelisk

7 Manse and garden

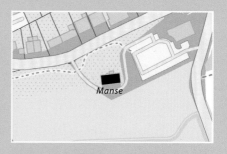

The present manse (minister's house) dates from 1805. Its predecessor was a much smaller building, located on the south side of the boundary wall of the manse garden just east of the church. It was built about 1740 and had two lower rooms and two upper rooms. The Rev William Bennet, an experimental horticulturist, built a glass structure and heightened the wall to make the chimney from the manse heat it, which allowed him to grow yams and pineapples. Evidence of the fireplace and some windows and a door still can be seen in this wall today.

His nephew and successor, also called the Rev William Bennet, ran a private boarding school in the manse. It cost sixpence per term with one penny extra for additions to the curriculum such as Latin.

The current manse is a Georgian 15-roomed building, extended by the Rev John Thomson's second wife, Frances. In 1821 she created a music room at its eastern end, without having asked the Presbytery for permission, perhaps because she planned to use it also for dancing. The stonework shown below makes the extension obvious.

Frances was an accomplished pianist, and her husband John Thomson a skilful violinist and flautist. They may have been preparing for the royal visit of George IV to Edinburgh in August 1822 – the first reigning monarch to visit Scotland for 150 years. Alas the King never visited the manse, but her husband was much involved in the royal visit.

The manse from the south

This resulted from his friendship with Sir Walter Scott, who stage-managed the entire visit. Scott and Thomson were close friends (see page 13) and they frequented each other's houses. In front of the manse with its views of the loch, Walter Scott sat and wrote some of his novel *Heart of Midlothian*: a rockery marks the very spot. Scott had also encouraged another friend, J M W Turner, to visit Edinburgh at the same time, and the result was many drawings in two Turner sketchbooks.

The manse garden features magnificent mature trees, some planted in the 19th century. Notable among these is the Waterloo walnut tree, perhaps planted at John Thomson's behest to celebrate the defeat of Napoleon in 1815. Black walnut is a rare species in Scotland and this magnificent specimen is probably the largest, and one of the most mature, in the country.

Upper: The rockery, manse garden
Lower: The Waterloo walnut tree

31

8 Garden Room & Millar Hall

The Kirk congregation today sees itself as a 21st century congregation, worshipping within a 12th century building. It has created new accommodation in the form of the Garden Room within the Millar Hall – a place of hospitality to welcome the stranger. Run by volunteers and open most days in summer, there is a warm welcome for everyone. One entrance is immediately to the left as you enter the gates to the Kirkyard, the other is via the manse garden.

Millar Hall and Garden Room

The Millar Hall was built thanks to a generous bequest from the late Moira Millar – an elder of the Kirk and a great supporter of its work. This small modern hall is close to the Kirk and enables the congregation to reach out to a wider community in new ways.

Visit information
The Garden Room is open in season (March to October) from 13.00 to 16.00 on Wednesday, Saturday and Sunday; and from 10.00 to 16.00 on Thursday and Friday. It is closed on Monday and Tuesday.

Millar Hall, exterior and interior

9 The glebe

In rural Scotland, landowners had to provide ministers with a glebe – at least five acres of arable land for the minister to graze his horse and grow crops to augment his meagre stipend.

When the church separated itself from the patronage of the landlords, every parish church fell heir to these lands. At Duddingston, the glebe is in several parts.

Today the Kirk lets part of the glebe situated behind the village for the grazing of horses. Another part of the glebe is let to Dr Neils Garden Trust, which maintains and develops the wonderful Dr Neils Garden: see page 34.

A third part of the glebe is being extended to accommodate local community groups offering a place of acceptance and welcome to cultivate the land in ecologically friendly ways. This area offers individuals places to mourn, and many families plant memorial trees, and find places to contemplate and pray while overlooking Duddingston Loch. It also includes the Path of Peace – made by local school children and challenging us to walk the path and commit our lives to peaceful ways.

Main: The Path of Peace
Inset: The dove; general view over the glebe

33

10 Dr Neils Garden

Nancy and Andrew Neil at work

Drs Andrew and Nancy Neil were a remarkable couple. Born respectively in 1919 and 1921, they both became general practitioners and were married in 1947. In addition to working together in a practice in Meadowbank (north of Holyrood Park), they shared an enthusiasm for gardening and travel. They combined these in caravanning holidays in France, Spain and Greece when they also collected plants and young trees.

In 1963 they lost their allotment to a car park and started looking for a new site to garden. A chance remark from one of their patients led to their taking on an area of glebe land between the Kirk and the loch known as the Calves Field.

This was a challenge indeed. There is a steep incline and though tilted towards the sun, the garden is also exposed to the prevailing wind. There is much rock in evidence, but it also underlies what is sometimes really shallow soil. The area had been used in the past for grazing geese and calves, but had never been cultivated.

But the Neils set to work, and after removing a mountain of spoil and general rubbish from just inside the gate, they cleared space in which they planted potatoes – where Thymes Square is today. They made a nursery plot to bring on tiny conifers, and Scots pines, larch, Norway spruce and Mediterranean cypress were grown from seed. Shelter belts of *Cupressus lawsonii* and *Escallonia* were planted.

As time went on, they made paths, steps and retaining walls using field stone found

Spring colour

Paved path

on site and much recycled material. Friends donated tools, sheds, garden seats and the splendid pair of terracotta urns near the top of the garden.

The Neils worked mostly alone – at weekends, and in the light evenings after work. It was essentially a private garden, but they encouraged family members, friends and patients to help. They were ahead of their time in prescribing gardening, rather than pills. They believed strongly in the health benefits of fruitful work in the fresh air.

In 1983 the garden featured in the BBC's *Beechgrove Garden* and in 1985 it opened for the first time under Scotland's Gardens Scheme. In 1991 Nancy and Andrew were jointly awarded the Queen Elizabeth the Queen Mother Medal by the Royal Caledonian Horticultural Society. Over the years the garden has featured in many newspaper and magazine articles, in tourist guides and in all three editions of *Scotland the Best*. In 2013 the garden celebrated its 50th birthday, and in late 2019 it appeared on BBC Scotland TV as part of Paul Murton's *Grand Tours*.

In 2005, Andrew and Nancy Neil died within a few months of each other. They had given up active involvement in the garden only in the last year or so of their lives, when they were already in their 80s. In 1998 responsibility had been devolved to Dr Neils Garden Trust, registered as a Scottish charity. A small management team works hard to earn income and to win funding for the care and development of the garden. In all this the Trust is most ably assisted by the gardener Claudia Pottier and her team of volunteers.

Claudia Pottier had worked in the garden with the Neils for two or three years before their retirement, and this apprenticeship helped her to pursue the Neils' aims and hopes for the garden – and still does. She brings a youthful energy and enthusiasm, and her more up-to-date horticultural training attracts a constant supply of volunteers of varying ages. Several of these have gone on to paid employment at the Royal Botanic Garden, Edinburgh and in other prestigious gardens.

Thymes Square

11 The Telford Bridge

This little bridge and pond is one of the garden's most popular features. Small children like to run across it, whooping as they reach the other side, and, rather more decorously, brides pose with their new husbands, reflected in the water beneath for their wedding-day photographs.

The pond was first dug by the Neils in 1974. It was enlarged and the bridge added in 1987. The Neils consulted a patient who taught engineering at Telford College, and he offered to construct the bridge as a project with his students. The wooden slats of the bridge have had to be replaced from time to time, and in 2018 the metal parts were superbly refurbished by one of the garden volunteers.

The garden's north-west corner had long been uncultivated before it was added to the garden in the 1990s. While working on this new space the gardener discovered the traces of a former pond. This has been reinstated, and a handsome timber viewing platform constructed for pond-dipping.

The Telford Bridge

12 The Physic Garden

When the Trust took the garden over, a ramshackle huddle of small storage sheds occupied a roughly circular area above the loch. The Trust raised some funding (chiefly from Awards for All) to build a new workshop and HQ close to the graveyard wall at the garden's western end. Once this was fitted with power, shelves and drawers, the old sheds were emptied and demolished.

The former shed site was cleared and levelled, and a Physic Garden planned in special commemoration of the garden's founders. The plan was based on eight interlocking petals forming a daisy shape. A narrow path divides the plot in two: the south-western portion contains plants used in Nancy's specialism (gyno-urinary medicine) and the north-eastern half reflects Andrew's special interest in ear, nose and throat complaints. (However, it was Andrew who delivered the babies.)

The eight small beds are outlined with low hedges of *Thuja*, itself a medicinal plant. An information panel inside a small hut identifies the plantings and explains how they were used in the past. The Physic Garden was opened formally in 2013 at a party to mark the Golden Anniversary.

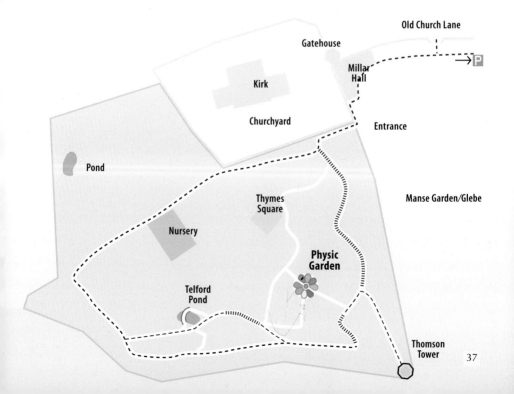

13 The Thomson Tower

This two-storey octagonal tower was designed in 1823 by the architect William Playfair for the Duddingston Curling Society. It commands an enviable view over Duddingston Loch and its use has always spanned both curling and artistic pursuits. The lower floor housed the curling stones, and was open to the weather to keep the stones at the correct temperature. The upper floor had windows and fireplace and allowed spectators to watch the game in comfort, with refreshments.

Curling is a sport in which players slide granite stones across ice into a target area. Two 4-person teams compete in what has been called 'chess on ice' because it demands strategy and accuracy. Unlike chess, however, teamwork is paramount.

The Duddingston Society was formed in 1795. After advocate James Millar joined in 1800 he created its motto *Sic Scoti: alii non aeque felices* – which can be loosely translated as 'This is how the Scots play: the others are not so lucky'.

Membership was marked by the presentation of a pair of stones and the purchase of a silver medal with the club's motto, and an image of men curling in front of Duddingston Kirk. Other clubs adopted variations of these medals and they have become highly collectable.

Above: Thomson Tower
Below: Skating on the loch, 19th century

The Duddingston club took a lead in documenting the rules of curling, and in 1804 it printed the rules and distributed them to its members. These rules quickly spread to other clubs, and the Duddingston rules still form the basis of the international game today. Sadly no curling takes place on the loch any more. The Curling Museum in the Tower has more information on the sport up to the present day.

Between 1805 and 1840, outside the curling season the upper meeting room was sometimes used as a studio by the Rev John Thomson: see page 13. The building became known as 'Edinburgh', and local people soon realised that when the minister was 'not at home but in Edinburgh' he was busy at his easel, rather than in the city.

The Tower was derelict for many years until 1977 when the Society for the Preservation of Duddingston Village raised funds from Canadian curlers, Historic Building Council, Edinburgh District Council and others, adequate to replace the roof. By the 1990s this second roof had perished, and after Dr Neils Garden Trust was formed in 1998, the focus was

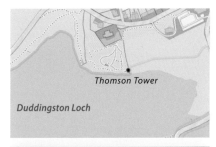

Thomson Tower

Duddingston Loch

Granite curling stone

on raising funds sufficient to restore the whole building and to revive its function. Funding came mainly from the Heritage Lottery Fund, Historic Scotland and the National Trust for Scotland. The renovated building was officially opened in 2009 and now hosts small meetings, workshops, exhibitions and parties.

South-east over Duddingston Loch

Viewed from the road through Holyrood Park, the loch provides a mirror image of the surrounding rocks and trees. Seen from its shores in Dr Neils Garden or the Bawsinch Nature Reserve, it is a place of peace and reflection.

Formed in a hollow probably cut by a combination of glaciers and glacial meltwater, Duddingston Loch is the largest natural freshwater loch in Edinburgh. It is shallow, with an average depth of only 2.2 m/7 ft, and its outflow into the Braid Burn is narrow. The result is that its rate of water exchange is slow. Combined with copious bird droppings, this means the loch has a high phosphorus content and in summer there are blooms of algae.

Naturally it provides the home for a classic vegetation succession from open water through reeds into woodland. Trees, especially birch, are gradually encroaching on the reed beds causing a management dilemma. Is it better to cut

Bittern standing tall for better camouflage

geese. In winter look out for the beautiful teal in the reeds along the south shore and the occasional Great crested grebe; through binoculars, you may see sedge warblers. Residents have reported many sightings of the elusive otter, mostly around dawn and dusk.

The human history of the loch is colourful as shown by names such as Hangman's Rock overlooking the north-west corner, and Murder Acre further west. The discovery in 1778 of the Duddingston Hoard (see page 49) and the cultivation terraces testify to human settlement dating from over 3000 years ago.

them down to preserve the reeds and hope to encourage the elusive bittern to settle and breed – they exploit these reeds for camouflage? Or should they allow the trees to grow, extending the base of the heronry? At the last count there were about 17 breeding pairs and 22 nests in tree-tops. To look down into their nests, climb onto Hangman's Rock.

Year-round the loch is home to mute swans, coots, mallards and more recently greylag geese and invasive Canada

More recently, Duddingston Loch was the scene of the world's first curling matches: see page 38. The cooler climate resulting from the so-called Little Ice Age created thick solid ice for both curling and skating. Skating was celebrated by Raeburn's famous painting: see page 56. Warmer winters, nature conservation management and a hawkish health and safety attitude mean that the loch is no longer used for winter sporting activities.

Across the loch to the Pentlands

15 Bawsinch Nature Reserve

Access steps

Boathouse

Glebe

Queen's Drive

Duddingston Low Road

Bawsinch and Duddingston Loch

Hide

Goose Green

Duddingston Road West

Innocent Cycleway

Duddingston Loch and its surrounding reedbeds and woodland had been given to the nation by William Askew of Ladykirk in 1923, and designated as a bird sanctuary in 1925. Much later, in 1971, the Scottish Wildlife Trust (SWT) bought the land adjacent to Bawsinch to protect and extend the bird sanctuary. The reserve today is an entirely natural-looking area with a mixture of trees, shrubs and wetlands hosting a variety of tree-nesting and roosting birds. The habitat is well suited to breeding, and it makes a haven for wildfowl and herons. The foresight and determination of the SWT volunteers are to be credited for this excellent result. Led by a forester, the late Colin MacLean, the area has grown a rich diversity of native British tree types including wild service tree (*Sorbus torminalis*) and Scottish natives such as the

quaking aspen (*Populus tremulus*). The diversity of trees was a creative way of blotting out the ugly mess made by human activity, including a car dump. Plants rare in Britain include tufted loosestrife, slender pondweed and needle spike rush.

More recently, SWT has prepared many small-scale habitats such as Goose Green for roosting geese, scrapes in pits to encourage sand martins to breed, flowering plants to attract butterflies and insects and water holes for a variety of wetland plants. The row of mature ash trees along the border with the Innocent railway provides a barrier to the sounds of the city, and also a roosting place for crow species.

This reserve is well worth a visit. The northern shore is open all year, reached via steps from the Duddingston entrance to Holyrood Park. Access to the southern shore is by prior arrangement, through a locked gate 🔒-o on Duddingston Road West. SWT members can borrow keys for access to the nearby hide, and anybody can sign up for one of the regular open days with an expert guide: see page 95 for details.

Tufted loosestrife

16 Reedbeds and Duddingston Hardings

The loch has extensive reedbeds, by far the largest area in the city. On the south-east and western shores, the reeds grow on marshes that merge into willow and poplar woodland, supporting many breeding species of wildfowl and heron.

The reeds were important to the history and economy of Duddingston long before it became a summer retreat for the affluent middle classes of Victorian Edinburgh. Reeds were dried and woven into a coarse cloth known as Duddingston Hardings. The weavers lived in primitive single-storey cottages in the Causeway, fitted with basic looms. In the 1760s at least 30 such cottage looms were operating, and weaving was an important source of employment in a village of about 500 people.

Hardings were used more for sacking than for clothing, being coarse in texture. Sacks were used to transport various goods – notably salt and coal – in smaller quantities for delivery into Edinburgh. Goods were sourced in Easter Duddingston, including the salt pans at Joppa, and taken into Edinburgh by Duddingston middlemen.

Horse-drawn transport was crucial in this 18th century development, and up to 36

Above and below: Reeds fringe the loch

horses were used to deliver goods in sacks or creels. However by the time of the Second Statistical Account of 1843, competition from more efficient mills elsewhere had decimated Duddingston's weaving industry, the reeds were no longer harvested and the population of the village had reduced to only 225..

17 Holyrood Park

Holyrood Park is the largest area of open space near the centre of Edinburgh. It covers 650 acres and contains three small lochs and a cluster of volcanic hills: see page 46. It belongs to the Crown and is both a Scheduled Ancient Monument and a Site of Special Scientific Interest, managed by Historic Environment Scotland: see page 95.

The park offers a huge variety of natural and human interest. Evidence of Bronze Age settlement and cultivation is still visible, and there are Iron Age defensive hilltop sites. It was a place of religion and sanctuary, and later quarry-ing and military training. Nature has retained its foothold on the six main hills: Salisbury Crags, Arthur's Seat, Nether Hill, Crow Hill, Whinny Hill and Dunsapie Crag.

The park is Edinburgh's largest area of unimproved grassland, with over 350 plant species. Attempts to restore lost species have been partly successful, most notably the sticky catchfly plant and the Northern brown argus butterfly. Before it was settled, it probably would have been more wooded with more boggy areas. It was transformed over many generations by clearance for cultivation, for building defences and for small settlements. A few decades ago, sheep were still grazed, but at a time when human use was rising rapidly the sheep presented management problems.

Sticky catchfly

From Duddingston, horizontal lines can clearly be seen on the slopes of Arthur's Seat and its neighbour, Crow Hill. These were constructed to help with cultivation, but when were they formed and why are they sometimes rig and furrow and sometimes terraces? About 3000 years ago, Bronze Age farmers probably devel-oped terraces on Crow Hill to provide thicker soils and to prevent crops slipping down the slopes.

The rig and furrow layouts are much later, probably of medieval origin. Both types of cultivation are evident on the eastern slopes of Arthur's Seat, which has 15 terraces with rig and furrows at a lower level. Others can be viewed from Prestonfield Golf Course – best seen in low light on a winter's afternoon.

Iron Age forts are prominent on the higher hills. A 20-acre site exists on Arthur's Seat, a slightly larger one on top of Salisbury Crags, and smaller ones on top of Dunsapie Crag and Samson's Ribs.

Salisbury Crags

Cultivation terraces on Crow Hill

Bronze Age flat axes were found on Dunsapie and a Roman intaglio (engraved finger ring) on Samson's Ribs.

The Holyrood sanctuary was one of the largest in Europe. From the 16th century it provided a place of safety for debtors otherwise at the mercy of their creditors and liable to imprisonment. The small community of debtors was known as Abbey Lairds. During the week they had to remain within the precincts to avoid arrest, but on Sundays they could wander more freely. Among them was the eccentric James Tytler: see page 67.

Quarrying became a significant activity, probably from the mid-16th century, for the construction of Holyrood Palace and the boundary wall around the Park ordered by James V. The remains of this period are still obvious at the whinstone quarry at the eastern end of Salisbury Crags and the large sandstone quarry at Camstone above those Crags.

The Radical Road was built by unemployed weavers in the 1820s, and still provides a bracing walk for those with a head for heights and wariness of rock falls. A rifle range in the Hunter's Bog area was in use for about a century from the 1850s.

Queen Victoria and Prince Albert made many changes to the Park, with extensive landscaping and drainage. The Queen's Drive was created as a high-level carriage route with excellent vistas. It roughly follows the perimeter of the Park and required cutting through rock on the southern side. They created two artificial lochs – St Margaret's and Dunsapie: see page 48.

The park became a place of sanctuary from the 12th century, functioning as a precinct to Holyrood Abbey. Whilst sanctuaries were common enough, the boundaries were normally tightly confined to the church or abbey.

18 Arthur's Seat

Duddingston lands and the village lie in the shadow of volcanic hills. This is as true now when the sun disappears from the village in the summer evenings as it was when a volcano was blasting away. It was active for up to 50 million years but became extinct about 320 million years ago. Its highest point is known as Arthur's Seat, but don't be fooled: King Arthur was never here. The name probably means Height of Arrows reflecting its role as an Iron Age hill fort. Its summit is at 251 m (823 ft).

Lava, ash, rocks and tiny particles known as tephra would have spewed out of the volcano's five vents and down its slopes. This produced a layered composition, visible in exposed areas such as the flat sections of Queen's Drive. The remnants of the five vents are known as Arthur's Seat, Lion's Haunch, Crow Hill, Whinny Hill and Dunsapie Crag, where the various volcanic materials solidified into rock.

Basalt columns, Samson's Ribs

Salisbury Crags were formed by hot rocks melting their way though the older sandstones and then cooling into these superb crags. Samson's Ribs are formed of lava cooled into hexagonal shapes; pieces frequently fall off and block the road.

At the time of the eruptions, Scotland lay at the equator on its long journey northwards from the southern hemisphere. It had a tropical climate with swamps and forests ultimately producing the coal seams which underlie parts of the city and its environs.

East over Arthur's Seat

Walk around the Queen's Drive (the upper road) to view the different rock types and envisage the might of the eruptions and spillage of the rocks down the slopes of the volcano which stood at least twice as high as the present hill.

Don't miss Hutton's Section at the Queen's Drive end of Salisbury Crags. This is one of the sites which convinced Dr James Hutton, the father of modern geology, that geological time was sempiternal. In 1645 Archbishop Ussher had calculated from biblical sources that the earth had begun as recently as 23 October 4004 BC. Hutton's fieldwork in Arran, Edinburgh and elsewhere led to his concept of deep time and his

North from Arthur's shoulder

revolutionary view that the earth was many millions of years old: 'we find no vestige of a beginning, no prospect of an end'. Nowadays, the estimate is about 4·5 billion years.

To the summit of Arthur's Seat

Of the many ascent routes, none is signed: before choosing any, please consider the weather conditions. In low cloud or mist there are occasional casualties – usually somebody who has become disoriented and by accident tries to descend over crags or cliffs. However, in good visibility this is a short and exhilarating ascent, mostly on easy slopes with a slight scramble near the top where you will be glad of sensible footwear. The summit views are superb, taking in the cityscape, surrounding hills and Firth of Forth to the north.

The route we recommend – the simplest to navigate – is shown on our map (back cover). Take the flight of steps just east of the car park, turn right along a short section of the Queen's Drive and bear left up a long grassy slope to approach the rocky summit area from the east. Unless you are competent with a map and compass, we suggest that you reverse your ascent route to descend safely.

19 Dunsapie Crag and Loch

Dunsapie Loch is shaped like a boomerang, and its artificial status is evident from the dam at its north-east corner. St Margaret's Loch is also man-made. Of the three lochs in the park only Duddingston – scooped out by a retreating glacier at the end of the last Ice Age – has a natural origin.

Dunsapie and St Margaret's Lochs were created when the Queen's Drive was built: see page 45. Queen Victoria and Prince Albert first stayed at Holyroodhouse in 1850 and they continued to be regular visitors until Albert's death in 1861. During this period they made many improvements both to the palace and its grounds – which included the whole of Holyrood Park.

The loch is kept topped up by water from Alnwickhill in the south of the city. It provides a home for mute swans, greylag geese, coots and several species of duck.

Dunsapie Crag towers above the inner curve of the loch. The crag is largely composed of a range of volcanic rocks that solidified around the vent.

On top of the crag are the remains of an Iron Age fort. The site is readily defensible, being protected on the north and west by almost sheer cliffs. From the south and east, the crag can be climbed by informal paths, steep in places but not difficult. The photo below, taken from the shoulder of Arthur's Seat, shows the northern and western cliffs dropping to the loch. It looks across the Firth of Forth to Fife, and to the volcanic plug of North Berwick Law distant on the right.

Above and below: Dunsapie Loch

20 Duddingston Hoard

Duddingston Hoard

In 1778 a hoard of over 40 Bronze Age weapons made between 1000 and 750 BC was discovered in Duddingston Loch. The occasion was the dredging of the loch bed for marl, a clay-like substance used to fertilise fields. In addition to spearheads, swords and dagger blades, the hoard contained a ring for a cauldron (or possibly a bucket handle). All of the weapons had been bent or broken, and some had been melted or burnt.

The hoard was the first donation received in 1781 by the Society of Antiquaries of Scotland, whose collection passed into public ownership in 1851, and it eventually became part of the National Museum of Scotland: the NMS now houses the hoard in its Early People gallery. However, it does not contain all of the bronze items originally found because the hoard was split between King George III, Sir Walter Scott and the museum. Nor does it contain the human

skulls and other human and animal bones dredged from the loch at the same time as the weapons.

For a long time, it was thought that the objects were scrap discarded by a bronze-smith. However, this would not explain why they had all been bent or broken – apparently deliberately. One theory is that the motivation was religious and that the hoard is the result of a 'weapon sacrifice'. It is also possible that the weapons had been captured from enemies and were broken to prevent them being used again, maybe in the afterlife. Possibly the human remains were those of defeated enemies.

The discovery of the hoard and the presence of remnants of a crannog (an inhabited artificial island) on the south side of Duddingston Loch seem to confirm the existence of a human settlement in the area in the late Bronze Age.

21 Miniature coffins

In June 1836, five schoolboys were out hunting rabbits on the north-eastern slopes of Arthur's Seat. They stumbled across a small cave, in which they found an exciting but mysterious treasure: 17 miniature carved wooden coffins arranged as two tiers of eight with a single coffin on top. Each coffin was about 4 inches long, and contained a tiny carved human figure with individual clothing and painted black boots.

Sadly, in the excited play fighting that followed their discovery, some of the figures were destroyed or lost, and others were later scattered among private collectors. In 1901 eight of the coffins were donated to the nation by a Mrs Couper, and they are on public display in the National Museum of Scotland. There are intriguing resources on the NMS website: see page 95.

There has long been speculation about the origin of these coffins, ranging from witchcraft to healing rituals to surrogate burials for people who had died elsewhere. The most plausible theory was advanced in the 1990s by Prof Sam Menefee working with Dr Allen Simpson, then a curator at the museum.

They examined the coffins, the figures and their clothing in forensic detail. The coffins had all been made from a single piece of wood, the tools and materials suggesting creation by a shoemaker. The cotton clothes and thread could be dated accurately, and could not have been buried before the early 1830s.

At that time, the scandal of Burke and Hare was fresh in everybody's memory. Their killing spree had begun when an elderly tenant of William Hare's boarding house had died owing him money. They found they could sell the corpse to Dr Robert Knox at his anatomy school for £12 (about £12,000 in today's money). This was incentive enough for them to murder 16 further victims. When arrested, Hare turned King's evidence and Burke was hanged in 1829, his corpse dissected in turn.

The fact that Burke and Hare sold 17 corpses seems a compelling coincidence in relation to 17 coffins, but that doesn't explain who made them, nor why. Ian Rankin wrote them into his 2001 thriller *The Falls*, and replica coffins made for its TV adaptation in 2006 can also be seen at NMS.

22 Park entrance

The Duddingston entrance to Holyrood Park is one of four: the two northern entrances are at Meadowbank and at Holyrood Palace, whereas the two on the south side are the Albert Gate (St Leonard's) and Duddingston Gate. Each has a lodge planned by Prince Albert when he was re-landscaping Holyrood Park about 1855-8. All share a similar style with steeply pitched roofs, Tudor-arched door surrounds and distinctive gables.

The design was by Robert Matheson, Clerk of Works for Scotland, and they all have inscribed date plaques with completion ranging from 1857 (Holyrood Lodge) to 1865 (St Leonard's). Only Holyrood and Duddingston Lodges are Grade-B listed, the other two being Grade-C – probably because they have been more extensively modified, especially their interiors. Duddingston Lodge's west wall proclaims 'VR 1858',

the same date as Meadowbank Lodge. The style is mock-Tudor, with corniced chimney flues set at an angle and a 'blind' arrowslit near the top of the roof.

The Park no longer has gates, but its gateposts are surmounted by decorative iron columns supporting hexagonal lanterns. On top of each lamp is a red gilded crown that reminds us of the Park's royal ownership.

At the eastern end of the car park, deeply screened by a tall hedge, is the flight of concrete steps whimsically known as 'Jacob's Ladder'. It forms the beginning of our suggested route up Arthur's Seat: see page 47.

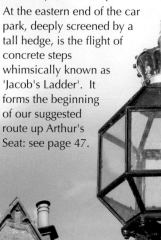

Below: Duddingston Lodge
Inset: Royal lantern

From the park entrance, walk up Old Church Lane and turn left at the Causeway. Pass the Sheep Heid's car park to reach its entrance around the corner. Now Duddingston's only pub, it is also one of Edinburgh's most famous. In times past Duddingston supported a dozen taverns, and probably some informal cottage-based brewing or distilling. This was when the village was a centre of weaving and other trades, and its population many times greater than at present.

The Sheep Heid claims to be the oldest surviving pub in Scotland. Its signs and

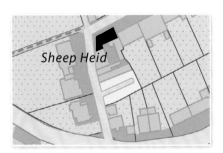

staff uniforms proclaim it was 'Established 1360' – a claim of doubtful meaning, so impossible to disprove. The concept of licensed premises had not arrived in the 14th century and selling alcoholic drink was largely unregulated.

Still, there has undoubtedly been a pub of some kind on the site for a very long time, and it has well-documented royal connections.

In the days when Scotland's monarchs spent some of their time at Craigmillar Castle, it was a stopping point on the way to Holyrood or Edinburgh. Mary Queen of Scots is said to have stopped by often and her son, James VI, was also a frequent visitor.

Theories differ about the origin of the pub's name. Sheep used to graze in the royal park and, at one time, were often slaughtered in Duddingston before the mutton was taken for sale in the Fleshmarket in the Old Town, just south of where Waverley Station now stands.

The heads were not in demand, so not worth taking to market. However, Duddingston residents were skilled at making dishes from them known as 'singed sheep heid' or 'sheep heid broth'. Alternatively the name may derive from the use of sheep heads as a kind of cobble or stepping-stone so people could pick their way through the mud of the Causeway itself. Whatever the origin, once King James VI had bestowed his royal gift (see page 54), the name stuck.

"Thrones' in the Sheep Heid

Over the years, the Sheep Heid has undoubtedly welcomed a great variety of interesting customers. It seems certain that, during the time they were camped nearby in 1745, the soldiers of Bonnie Prince Charlie's army will have enjoyed a drink in the pub. In the 19th century visits by Sir Walter Scott and later Robert Louis Stevenson gave it a literary clientele. Perhaps Sir Walter's friend, the Rev John Thomson, may have visited, although there have

Her Majesty
The Queen
Visited The
Sheep Heid Inn
On the
6th July 2016

been long periods in the past when Kirk and pub were at odds.

The tradition of royal patronage has been maintained. In July 2016 the current Queen had dinner at the inn following a day at the races at Musselburgh. Unlike Mary and James, she made no use of the skittles alley. However the pub has commemorated her visit with 'thrones' and a wall plaque.

The building has a complicated history with alterations being made over two and a half centuries. Its interesting past and the charm of the pub continue to attract visitors to Duddingston.

24 The snuff box

Snuff is finely powdered tobacco, usually inhaled by sniffing from the back of the hand. It delivers a swift hit of nicotine. Its use seems to have originated in Brazil but was well established in the Caribbean by the time of Columbus's voyages. A Spanish friar brought some back to Spain in 1493. Snuff taking is no longer common, but its use was very widespread in Europe from the 16th to the 19th century.

Replica of the original snuff box

James VI was strongly opposed to tobacco smoking, describing it in 1604 as 'loathsome to the eye, hateful to the nose, harmful to the braine, dangerous to the lungs'. However, he was more tolerant of tobacco in the form of snuff.

In 1580 he donated to the Sheep Heid an ornate snuff box shaped like a ram's head. The ram was of a dun-faced breed, common at the time but now extinct. Originally there was a golden ball at the tip of each of the horns, and its eyes were made from semi-precious stones. Apparently it hung from the wall by a golden chain, perilous as this sounds. The snuff box remained on the site for 300 years before it was sold at auction to the Earl of Rosebery whose family still keeps it at Dalmeny House. The photo shows the 19th century replica in dark wood with glass eyes that is normally on display behind the bar.

It may be that this snuff box was the origin of the pub's name, or perhaps King James's gift commemorated a name that was already well established. Either way, the pub has been known as the Sheep Heid ever since to visitors – albeit many locals call it the Sheepie. The famous head has certainly featured on external pub signs in various guises over the centuries. The current version, highly stylised, was created as part of the pub's 2019 refurbishment, and contrasts with older, more representational examples.

25 Skittles alley

The Sheep Heid contains one of Scotland's few remaining pub skittle alleys. This is also one of the oldest, having been built in 1882 on the site of the old stable block.

Skittles is a game with many variants and a long history. It may have originated in ancient Egypt, perhaps as much as 5000 years ago. It has long been popular as a pub game throughout the UK and Ireland, whilst a different version is played in German-speaking countries. The phrase 'beer and skittles' clearly links the game to leisure time spent in pubs. It was the basis of the modern game of ten-pin bowling.

The Sheep Heid alley is in no way automated. Players set up the skittles by hand in a self-contained wood-panelled space, then propel the heavy balls along a wooden lane to try to knock them down. The alley can be hired for exclusive use for the evening or by the hour, and it is popular for children's parties.

Trotters Club at skittles in 1904

Over the years this skittles alley has been a meeting place for clubs and informal groups. Most famous of these is the Trotters Club, founded by three journalists in 1882. The club had a literary aspect, with a strong emphasis on sociable dinners, skittles and outings. The photo above shows a wide range of ages and suggests a social mix, but it was an all-male club. Membership declined after World War 1 and the club folded. It was revived in 1943 and the club started admitting women in 2000. For its more traditional members, this was a step too far and the Trotters now survive only as an archive housed in the Kirk.

Skittles alley in 2014

26 Sheep Heid memorabilia

Take some time to look at all that is on the walls inside the Sheep Heid. There's a wide range of interesting objects – photos of old Edinburgh jostle with clocks, bills, old maps and even a royal portrait. According to the price list on the stairs, you can buy a pint of beer for a shilling (£0.05) but only if you had visited in 1946. There are also two paintings closely related to village history.

The first hangs in a passageway – a framed reproduction of Henry Raeburn's 'The Reverend Robert Walker skating on Duddingston Loch'. (The attribution to Raeburn has been disputed, but is now accepted by most experts.) The original oil painting was created about 1790, and was largely unknown until it was bought for the national collection in 1949 for £525. It has since become Scotland's best-known portrait, generally referred to as 'the skating minister'. The original hangs in the National Gallery of Scotland on The Mound.

It shows a romanticised loch with an improbably rugged Arthur's Seat and the minister skating effortlessly, arms folded. Walker had learned to skate as a boy on

Reproduction of the 'skating minister' in the pub

Dutch canals when his father was minister of the Scots Kirk in Rotterdam. He was a member of the Edinburgh Skating Club, the world's oldest, which used Duddingston Loch and held an annual dinner where the local dish of sheep's head and trotters was served. Walker became minister of the Canongate Kirk (and therefore chaplain to the Palace of Holyroodhouse) in 1784. Although an establishment man, he was also a true Enlightenment figure who persuaded the Presbytery of Edinburgh to campaign against slavery.

Around the pub walls

Near the main entrance is a painting of the Battle of Prestonpans, fought on 21 September 1745 between Jacobite* forces and the government army. The painting shows the view north-east over the battlefield from Birsley Brae, near Tranent. Bonnie Prince Charlie had landed in the Hebrides in July 1745 and quickly raised an army from among the Highland clans. They marched south and the Prince entered Edinburgh unopposed on 17 September. On 19 September he and his generals held a council of war in a house on the Causeway: see page 68. In the meantime Sir John Cope, commander of the government forces, had sent his troops by sea to Dunbar where they also arrived on 17 September.

Victorian skating boots

The armies first engaged briefly on 20 September near Prestonpans, but very early the next morning the Jacobites moved to better positions. Despite being outnumbered, within half an hour the Jacobites had prevailed. Many government troops panicked and fled, and they suffered four times as many casualties as those of the Jacobites. Sir John Cope was later court-martialled but acquitted. From the Jacobite viewpoint, the early victory at Prestonpans encouraged them to pursue an over-ambitious campaign that finished in disaster at Culloden in 1746.

See page 94 for more about the Jacobites.

The Battle of Prestonpans; Bonnie Prince Charlie (inset)

OLD CHURCH LANE

Old Church Lane is in strong contrast with the village's only other street, the Causeway: see page 64. Most of its houses date from the period 1816-30, so they are more homogeneous in their ages and styles. Unlike the Causeway, nearly all the houses are on its northern side and are even-numbered. The south side has a superb high stone wall running unbroken for 200 m/650 ft from the Kirk entrance to the main road, interrupted only by ironwork gates that give access to the Manse.

Decorative ironwork

Excluding the Kirk, Old Church Lane is entirely residential, and always has been. The only exception is number 22, Church Hill Cottage. This former weaver's cottage was rebuilt to serve as the village school. When the Kirk Session visited in February 1810 it already had 45 scholars and they proposed an extra storey for 'the schoolmistress to teach the girls needlework'. Many other improvements include a porch, plastering and extra windows were authorised to deal with the likely increase in numbers. By 1811, however, the school had moved to a building near Duddingston Mills. Church Hill Cottage remained the schoolmaster's house until 1827 when there was a public auction.

Old Church Lane was originally known as South Street, later as Church Lane. The 8th Earl of Abercorn created this new road at about the same time that he started to lay out its housing by selling plots of land. Many of the houses were

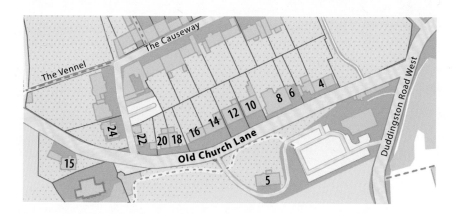

used as holiday homes by affluent citizens of Edinburgh seeking the rural pleasures of Duddingston in summer and skating or curling in winter. With the exception of Church Hill Cottage and the two 20th century houses at its western end, the houses on this road were mainly built within a period of only 15 years, followed by the addition of two semi-villas in about 1860.

The six villas in the eastern part of the road are numbered 4 to 16, and originally the houses must all have looked very similar – only the stylish Georgian house at number 10 is a bungalow: see photo below. The rest all have two storeys, and their symmetrical facades feature a central main door with a single window bay on either side. Over the last two centuries, many modifications and extensions have disguised their underlying similarity. Nevertheless all six of these late Georgian houses are Grade-B Listed, as is the manse opposite (number 5): see page 30.

To see this underlying similarity, from the pavement look at number 14 (Lochside House) and compare it with number 16 to its left. Number 16 was clearly built to the same design, with the two-storey bay window on its left side added later. Look also at number 12, which

Victorian mock-castle detail on number 8

resembles number 14 closely except that the house is unusually tall, its upper storey ceilings as high as the lower.

The windows of number 12 feature astragals that divide them into 12 panes. All the Georgian villas would originally have had astragalled windows because techniques for creating large panes of glass had not yet been developed. Windows would later gain larger panes, but nearly every window on the street is still timber sash and case.

10 Old Church Lane

Moving east, look also at numbers 8 and 6, formerly a single villa called Glen Arthur. In Victorian times it was embellished with a gothic-style tower with bay windows and engraved crosses. The roofline was adorned with a weather-vane and crow-stepped gables and stone consoles added to its windows. It was divided horizontally into two dwellings in the 1960s, and extensions were later built onto both sides. Nonetheless, originally it would have closely resembled number 14. To its east is number 4, the Home House: see page 63. On the other side of the road stands the former beadle's cottage, recently restored.

Further west on Old Church Lane is a symmetrical pair of semi-villas: numbers 18 and 20 date from about 1860 and they look thoroughly Victorian. The clues are in the front corner ashlars (dressed corner stones), stone bevels around the windows and the continuous roofline cornice. Despite the 30-year gap, they look comfortably in keeping with their neighbours.

Beyond number 22 and across the Causeway stand the street's only 20th century houses: number 24 (Gateside) is on the right and dates from 1907, opposite number 15 (Craigneuk) which dates from 1920. The final house with an address in Old Church Lane is inside the Park – number 32, better known as Duddingston Lodge: see page 51.

The Georgian and Victorian houses exhibit a wealth of interesting detail. The walls are made of attractive sandstone in a range of heights, probably quarried at Craigmillar. In its rough, undressed state it is known as rubble – whereas ashlars are regular stones with a smooth finish. Sandstone walls throughout the village enhance its sense of enclosure. Number 4 has its walls completely harled to protect the soft stone from erosion.

Subtle colours in rubble wall

The rustic stone has subtle colour variations, and mature trees are everywhere – deepening the sense of a rural enclave.

There is a range of wrought iron railings and balconies. A prevalent motif is a vertical feature with encircled flower set between decorative heart shapes above and below: see also page 58. This is best seen in the railings outside number 10, or at the left side of number 14.

Heart-shaped motif

28 Wall plaque

On the corner opposite the Kirk, this square bronze panel is inset into the wall, with the inscription: 'Under the seat beside the water makes a home for a' Jock Tamson's bairns'. This refers clearly to the village and Kirk where John Thomson (Jock Tamson) preached, which lies in the shadow of Arthur's Seat, on the edge of Duddingston Loch. The idiom 'We're a' Jock Tamson's bairns' is still used today in Scotland: see page 13.

The central motif was inspired by local horse chestnut trees that have provided conkers for generations of Duddingston children. The fox and squirrel represent the rich local fauna, and the lark (or 'laverock') in the tree is a reference to its appearance in *The Heart of Midlothian*, the novel that Walter Scott was working on in the garden of the manse.

Many historical references are handwritten into the banners woven into the branches, including the Jacobite planning of the Battle of Prestonpans in the Causeway, Duddingston Curling Club rules, the Rev John Thomson, R L Stevenson's poem *Duddingstone*, the Sheep Heid Inn, the 12th century Kirk and the Bronze Age settlements.

Bronze panel, Old Church Lane

The panel forms half of a two-part installation commissioned in 1999 by Edinburgh City Council and the National Trust for Scotland from artist Tim Chalk who lives on Old Church Lane. Its counterpart is the bench below the gatehouse: see photo below.

The seat has a bronze inset with the legend 'Fire made the seat beside the water' referring to the volcanic origin of Arthur's Seat beside the loch. It depicts two geese (Canada and greylag) and a goldeneye duck among the reeds beside the loch, with a suggestion of Arthur's Seat behind.

Bench beneath the gatehouse

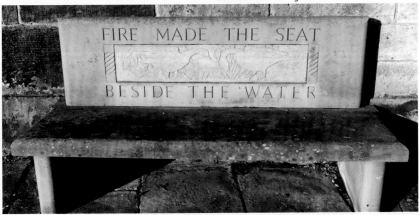

29 12 Old Church Lane

Number 12 is one of the Georgian villas whose elegant frontage has remained largely unchanged since it was built in 1829. The plot of this house was bought from the Earl of Abercorn in January 1813 by the Rev John Thomson, then minister of the Kirk: see page 12. The sale was subject to the condition that within two years a house be built on the land. This provision was to ensure that a building was put up of sufficient value to provide ample security for the feu duty (ground rent). In the event, John Thomson made no move to construct a house and the Earl seems to have taken no action to enforce it.

So the plot was still empty in 1828 when Thomson sold it to John MacKenzie, a retired soldier and former major in the 46th Regiment of Foot. MacKenzie began work and construction seems to have been completed in the following year. The architect is not known, but the house was fitted out and furnished by Gordon Brown, cabinet-maker, who was based in Buccleuch Place. It is built on a large scale, being considerably taller than the other villas.

Sadly, the major had very little time to enjoy his house: he died in September 1830 at the age of 55. The house, then named Duddingston Lodge, was advertised for sale immediately but without success. It was rented to several tenants before becoming the property of Dr William Browne, an important figure in the history of the treatment of mental illness. He was the superintendent of the Crichton Asylum in Dumfries and pioneered a number of humane therapies. He sold the house in 1878 for the sum of £755.30.

A succession of owners followed who, no doubt, adapted it to meet the needs of their times. However, they made very few changes to its outward appearance. As a result, from the street, number 12 gives a very good idea of how all of the adjacent houses must have looked when first built.

12 Old Church Lane

30 The Home House

By 1817 John Henderson, an innkeeper, had built a house on the two adjoining plots now known as 4 Old Church Lane. Its facade was symmetrical, having a central door with a window on each side and three windows above, very similar to neighbouring houses. Over the years its residents have been people from a wide social mix, ranging from those 'in trade' to members of the professions and arts.

John Purves, a smith of Broughton Street, bought the house in 1818, and it was later sold several times. After 1855, it was rented out: an early tenant was John Wilson, a student who later became the medical officer at Wanlockhead Mines, Dumfriesshire. A handsome memorial to his family stands in Duddingston graveyard.

In 1877 Henry Seton, consultant veterinarian, bought the house. He was active within the Kirk and community, and on his death in 1889 he left his estate to good causes. The new owner was John Young of Young & Saunders, grocers in Queensferry Street. About this time a single-storey extension was added to the east.

In 1900 the house was purchased to make a home for the children of Church of Scotland missionaries serving abroad – becoming known as the Home House. The extension was enlarged and an upper storey added. Later a schoolroom annex with sickroom and bathroom was added at the western end. Having survived both World Wars, it was sold to the Livingstone Home for Friendless Girls and then to the Scottish Female Domestic Servants Association, for use as a retirement home.

In 1962 the house was given to the Edinburgh and Leith Old People's Welfare Society, but by 1991 it could no longer meet modern safety standards. A family bought it and restored it to domestic use. Among other improvements, they commissioned two decorative ironwork balconies for the eastern extension that precisely match the original three, and a new pair of gates at the west end.

Home House, 4 Old Church Lane

31 The Causeway

The Causeway has many more homes than Old Church Lane, and its population is four times greater, with over 100 residents compared with the latter's 25 or so. The houses are also much more varied in age, style and size. The oldest are weavers' cottages dating from the early 18th century, and the most recent is the traditional-looking number 25, completed in 1999.

Weavers' cottages, with Sycamore Bank behind

Over three centuries, new buildings have ranged from large villas to tenement flats, from terraced houses to working men's cottages. With the exception of the pub, the Causeway is now essentially residential.

However, it used to be the heart of the village economy, with about 30 cottage-based weaving looms, several taverns, shops and a post office. It was cobbled, at first probably with crude stones and sheep skulls set into the mud, later with stone setts. The name Causeway is a corruption of the Scots word *causey* meaning cobbled street, which derives from an obsolete Norman French word *caucie* (variously spelled).

Number 40

the engraving (page 64) and in the photo on the left. The contrast between living conditions then and now is enormous.

Three large villas, Bella Vista, Hawthorn Brae and Hillside (44) were constructed on the north side. They are eclectic in design, set well back from the road and were built for very affluent families. For more about Hawthorn Brae, see page 70. To the right of Hillside is number 42, a handsome Grade-B listed house dating from the late 18th century.

Several cottages survive from the era when weavers lived and worked in them. The cottage at number 50 has been sensitively restored using traditional-looking materials, but upgraded to 21st century standards of interior comfort. Three such cottages were combined into a single house at number 40, shown in

On the south side stands Jane Cottage, dating from the early 19th century but rebuilt in 1900 when its distinctive bay windows with balconies were added. The old photo below shows them covered in fresh snowfall. Almost opposite are the two fine Grade-B two-storey houses at numbers 58 and 60, Poplar Bank and Dairy Cottage.

Jane Cottage

Numbers 4 and 6 the Causeway, former shops

The Bonnie Prince Charlie house is described on page 68. To its right are houses that show traces of their former role as shops. Above the doors of numbers 4 and 6, in good light you can still discern most of the lettering WINES TEAS & SPIRITS, and GROCER is very clear on the sheltered gable wall. The village postbox in the wall of number 2 is all that remains of the former post office.

Towards the western end of the Causeway, new forms of housing appeared in the 19th century. On the south side was built a large cottage (33) and a small block of flats (35-39). The ground floor apartments have their own front doors, whilst the upper flats are reached through a common stairway. On the north side, a three-storey tenement (52-56) provided a further 12 homes.

Development continued in the 20th century. At number 41 a three-storey tenement proudly proclaims its date as '1929'. Different again is the last of the Causeway's big mansions, Maitland Lodge, an arts and crafts house set at the north edge of its huge plot. At one time it was entered through a gate on Old Church Lane, but later it became 21 the Causeway. Charlescote is a smaller house of similar vintage at number 12: see page 69. Adjacent is a small enclave of seven houses built by Miller Homes in 1962-3.

The original owners of Hawthorn Brae kept their plots on the south side vacant as a village drying green. In the 1970s three modern houses (numbers 27, 29 and 31) were built on this space, the work of Guy Oddie, professor of architecture at Edinburgh University. Further left is a narrow lane leading to the three Abercorn Cottages: see photo opposite. These attractively restored working men's cottages are unique in the Causeway, which boasts homes in a wide range of styles.

An interesting character lived in the Causeway in the late 18th century. James Tytler (1745-1804) had lodgings there

Abercorn Cottages

Sadly, his success was soon over-shadowed by the exploits of Lunardi, an Italian balloonist, at St Andrews. After 1790 he became involved in radical politics, publicly denouncing the House of Commons and urging people to withhold taxes. He was charged with seditious libel and in 1793 he fled to Salem, Massachusetts. After 11 years there he died, seemingly drowned after a drunken expedition to borrow a candle at night.

Tytler was a remarkable man: at different times he scraped a living as chemist, surgeon, printer, poet, journalist and editor. It was Robert Burns who in 1788 referred to him as 'that odd being, Balloon Tytler' – 'balloon' being a colloquial term of contempt. In his lifetime Tytler was considered a failure and subjected to ridicule, but in hindsight many of his achievements deserve respect. Ferguson's excellent biography paints a more sympathetic picture of this amazing man: see page 95.

Grand Edinburgh Fire Balloon

with a washerwoman, together with his five children. He was spectacularly talented and energetic, but financially disastrous. Not long before (1774) he had been an 'Abbey Laird' – a debtor taking refuge: see page 45. An early hasty marriage forced him to abandon his education, and when he was trying to support his family he turned to prolific writing. During his Duddingston years (probably 1777-1784), he edited and wrote about three-quarters of the second edition of Encyclopaedia Britannica using his landlady's upturned wash tub as a desk. It was steady work, but seriously underpaid at under one pound a week. He lived in great poverty while producing over 9000 pages.

It was research for an appendix that sparked his interest in air balloons, and he became the first man in Scotland to take to the air. His Grand Edinburgh Fire Balloon flight from Abbey Mount to Restalrig took place in August 1784.

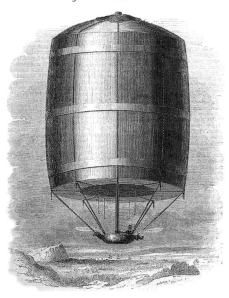

32 Bonnie Prince Charlie house

The building at 8-10 the Causeway has been known as Bonnie Prince Charlie's House only since the 20th century. It is where the Prince held his council of war before the Battle of Prestonpans in 1745. He did not sleep there, but in the greater luxury of Holyrood Palace. However, he made his battle plans there with clan leaders. For a painting of the battle and its outcome, see page 57.

In this house on 19th September 1745 PRINCE CHARLES EDWARD STUART held his Council of War before the battle of Prestonpans

The house is one of the oldest in the village. It may have been built as early as 1721 and was certainly in place well before 1745. Originally it was Abercorn Tavern, one of a dozen or more taverns in the Causeway. For some time it was owned by the Hay family, who owned the adjacent shops and post office. The house features a large 'smoking chimney' for curing finnan haddock. The flue starts in no 10 the Causeway and ends in the attic of no 1 Abercorn Cottages.

The house fell into disrepair in the early part of the 20th century and was rescued in 1962 by Trustees of the recently created Society for the Preservation of Duddingston Village (SPDV). Funds for its restoration quickly reached £500 as a result of donations from the village and beyond. The Society then sold it for £1200 to Edinburgh University School of Architecture which then restored it, renovating its main façade and including a stone plaque to commemorate its role in 1745. The conversion into two dwellings was completed in 1970.

On the occasion when SPDV was established, a photograph shows Sir Compton Mackenzie – writer, actor, soldier and spy – presenting a bronze death mask of Bonnie Prince Charlie to Willliam Cruickshank. It is one of four made in Rome at the time of the death, of which only two survive. Cruickshank passed it on to Sydney Byrne Stewart, an artist and sculptor who lived in this house at the time. Finally it was given to the Scottish National Portrait Gallery where it is still on display. A recent facial reconstruction shows a slight twist to the prince's mouth, suggesting that he may have died of a stroke.

Upper: Inscription above doorway
Lower: Bonnie Prince Charlie house

33 Charlescote and its wall

The attractive arts and crafts house at 12 the Causeway is called Charlescote. It dates from the early 20th century and is set well back from the road.

Charlescote

However its boundary wall tells of an earlier house that reached much farther forward, even more than its neighbour, the Bonnie Prince Charlie house. Look for the filled in apertures in the stone wall of Charlescote: the photo below looks north along the wall and you can count three blocked up windows; the doorway and two windows beyond are not in shot, but are still clearly visible on the wall itself.

Confirmation comes from the Victorian engraving below which also faces north up the Causeway. The three women are outside the Bonnie Prince Charlie house, with a drying area to its left. The two-storey house to its left extends to the pavement, and its doorway has three windows to the right and two to the left – exactly matching the apertures visible in the boundary wall to this day.

Boundary wall of Charlescote

North up the Causeway, 19th century engraving

34 Hawthorn Brae

Hawthorn Brae is a fine example of the opulent houses that were built in Duddingston during the Victorian period when the village was seen as a picturesque, semi-rural retreat from the city. It is one of the largest villas built in the Causeway during the 19th century, and the only house in the village that is Grade-C listed. Building began about 1820, similar to the Georgian villas of Old Church Lane. However, in the mid and later years of the century it was greatly extended and altered. Nonetheless it retains a fine coherent appearance, commanding the Causeway from its location high above the road.

The house is very large, having two main floors, an attic and basement. Its porch features Tuscan columns approached by a curved staircase, with above it a stone balcony with balustrades and urns. Uniquely, it has two impressive gateways with wrought iron gates and a pedestrian entrance inscribed with 'Hawthorn Brae'.

The original owners (named Scott) also owned the adjacent kitchen garden, connected by a gate. This has now become the DCS community vegetable garden: see page 77. The Scotts were clearly both wealthy and very concerned about their amenity. They purchased five plots on the south side of the Causeway to safeguard their view. This approach was very successful, and no development took place on these sites until well into the 20th century.

In 1897 the house was given to a Christian organisation as a respite home for missionaries, and was later leased to the Church of Scotland. Institutional use meant that many internal partitions had been installed. These were removed when the house reverted to being a private home.

Hawthorn Brae

Lochside Cottage (number 66) lies just south of the Vennel, and is one of six Grade-B listed buildings in the Causeway. The other five are the Sheep Heid, numbers 58 and 60, number 42 and the Bonnie Prince Charlie house. Before the construction of Old Church Lane, the only access to the Royal Park was from the Causeway, down the Vennel beside this garden.

This is where Nicholas Fairbairn lived with his parents when, as a young man, he and William Cruickshank founded the Society for the Preservation of Duddingston Village. The house was built in 1787 by the 8th Earl of Abercorn, perhaps as a factor's house. Its original stairway was replaced by a curving Regency staircase with delicate ironwork and a polished wooden handrail brought from a house in East Lothian. After it was sold in 1927, the west-facing wing with bow windows was added, probably to enhance its views over the loch. The photo above dates from 1965 when the Society was six years old.

From the park, the main house can barely be seen, but there is a fine view of the pantiled stone outhouse built into its western boundary wall. Dating from the 18th century, this had once been a tavern, one of many in the village. It tapers to the north, and its stonework clearly testifies to two or more phases of building. With its two sets of chimneys and many windows, it may be the most grandiose garage in the village.

Stone outhouse near the park entrance

36 Community Land

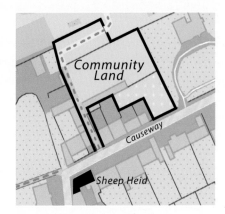

The story of the Community Land starts with Chrissie McNiven, an early secretary of the Conservation Society (then known as the Society for the Preservation of Duddingston Village). She died in 1979 and wanted to bequeath her house (14 Old Church Lane) to the village. Following advice, she bequeathed it to the National Trust for Scotland, who sold it and invested the income.

The Community Land comprises (from north to south) the paddock (formerly stabling for horses), the former tennis court, the vegetable garden and the byre. In 2001 the garden, along with Dairy Cottage, was bought by the National Trust for Scotland using the McNiven bequest. It was then leased to the Conservation Society for community use.

Many neighbours helped to clear the overgrown brambles and self-seeded trees and organised community events in the garden. A marquee was bought and set up in the old tennis court each summer, allowing events to take place regardless of the weather.

The NTS decided that they could use the McNiven bequest for their general funding and initiated procedures to sell the community garden for housing. They subsequently agreed to sell it to the

Former tennis court, now a village green

Conservation Society. Although the asking price seemed a vast sum for a small charity, residents and friends contributed generously; the full amount was raised and the purchase completed in 2014.

Major changes followed: now that the garden belonged to the community, much more use could be made of it by local residents and the general public and more events were organised. Management was delegated to the Community Land Group, a subgroup of the DCS Board. Since 2014, the group has worked with an architect and engineers to produce designs for a refurbished byre and to obtain planning permission. They have built two (donated) greenhouses and rebuilt part of the main access path, put up signs to welcome and inform visitors and generally made the site more welcoming and easier to find.

The old tennis court has become the new village green. Residents, friends and guests gather there for a range of events each year, such as the midsummer breakfast, the village party, Apple Day,

Lantern Festival

bonfire night and the winter party, as well as informal get-togethers and barbecues. Two Lantern Festivals were held in 2017 and 2018, with spectacular processions through the village and the launch of a lantern moon over the loch.

The Community Land provides a space for producing healthy food, as well as composting and recycling organic material. More important, it brings the community together in a place where people work alongside each other while socialising. It is a unique asset for an urban village.

Former paddock, leading to the Field

37 The field

In 2011 the Community Land Group (CLG) noticed the previous tenants of the field pulling up their fences. They had kept horses there for 40 years, but were moving out because of a major rent rise. They had leased it from Edinburgh Council, who were keen to work with local residents to set up a community lease with the agreed aims of habitat restoration and public access. The Council had no objection to the CLG keeping a few hens (although no other livestock) and they welcomed the plan to establish an orchard.

Rowan berries in the field

Only eight years later, the results of much labour are visible to the many visitors. The first task was to set up a path network, followed by installing six simple benches (designed by the group) and all with different views. Then planting could begin – apple and pear trees to form an orchard with native trees and shrubs in the western, woodland part.

The planting of at least 1000 trees and 2000 shrubs will have had a positive impact on air quality and carbon capture: their cooling effect reduces ozone formation and they absorb air pollutants into their leaves. They also increase biodiversity by providing shade and nutrition to a wide variety of insects, and they provide shelter and nesting sites for birds.

About one third of the area was set aside for restoration as a wildflower meadow, to be mowed once or twice a year and with wild flowers planted in patches to

support more diversity and food sources for pollinators. The results are obvious in the range of plants and animals now found, such as damselflies, hedgehogs, barn owls and cowslips. Several hundred people visit the field each month – walking their dogs, taking children to see the hens, having picnics and enjoying the views.

As you enter the field from the paddock, the orchard spreads up the south-facing slope. The first apple trees were planted in 2012 and there are now some 106 apple varieties, 10 pear varieties and a quince. A separate lower section contains plum and damson trees. The range includes over 50 Scottish and heritage varieties of apple. Many of the trees have been grafted by the team over the years. Each year's harvest is celebrated with an Apple Day, with apple tasting and juice-making.

Apple tree in fruit

All this has required a massive amount of work, and in addition to many regular volunteers, an Edinburgh University student society called the Dirty Weekenders arrives two or three times a year. They come in groups of 20 to 40, and do huge amounts of heavy work such as moving sacks of sand from the street up to the field or raking the mown grass from the meadow. Work days, and especially lunches around the big table, are social events, building friendships and sharing this beautiful piece of land.

38 The byre

The byre is the former milking parlour for Grant's dairy, probably dating from the early 20th century. Until 2005 when the roof was removed by the National Trust for Scotland (NTS), the old stalls were still visible, along with the milk pipes and feeding troughs. Many of these troughs now grace gardens in the village.

Until World War 2, cows were milked here after being driven down the Causeway from nearby fields – probably where the houses of Meadowfield now stand. The milkman, Willie Grant, lived in Dairy Cottage and stored the milk (and little bottles of orange juice much beloved by village children) in sheds just behind the old house. He retired in the 1970s, and built a greenhouse behind the sheds to grow tropical lilies. He also renovated several classic cars in the byre.

The byre was acquired by the NTS in 2001 and immediately declared unsafe, so it could not be used. Following removal of the roof, the building quickly deteriorated until it was bought by the DCS along with the Community Land. Volunteers cleared out the building, stabilised the walls and now use it for various small community events, including celebrations, film nights and

Entrance to the byre

tool sharpening days. In 2018, Portobello Tool Library volunteers built a shelter for lunches and to permit working in bad weather.

The byre will benefit from further temporary improvements to enable more use for fundraising events, leading up to full refurbishment when funds allow. This will include toilets, a room for community activities and a workshop with secure tool store.

Cows in the Causeway

39 Vegetable garden

The vegetable garden of today was originally the kitchen garden for Hawthorn Brae: see page 70. The garden turned into a rubbish dump after the house became a children's home. It was bought in the 1970s by a local resident and allowed to grow wild, with a fox's den, teeming bird life and rampant brambles.

In the 1990s, parts were cleared to grow flowers, and later a basket willow plantation was established. When the NTS bought it in 2001, volunteers again cleared the ground and built paths and compost boxes. They planted soft fruit, vegetables, herbs and flowers, with apples, plums and cherries along the walls.

Access staircase

In recent years there has been valuable construction work. To combat local flooding a major drain was laid across the garden. A joiner-built staircase provides access from the rest of the Community Land. The original wrought iron and timber door from Hawthorn Brae has been refurbished, as were the dilapidated brick walls.

The management is entirely communal, with volunteers donating their time and taking some of the produce, supported by small investments by the DCS from time to time, mainly for equipment. Running costs are otherwise covered by donations, sales of vegetables (including a small seasonal vegetable scheme) and donations at events.

After heated debate, it was decided that the garden should be organic (though not certified). Locally produced compost, along with organic fertiliser, keeps the soil rich and productive. The vegetable garden brings benefit to the community, through home-grown vegetables – which have more micro-nutrients and fewer toxins than commercially-grown crops – and healthy, sociable exercise for the many volunteers.

40 Duddingston House

Duddingston House was built for James Hamilton, 8th Earl of Abercorn (1712–1789). With the Jacobite risings safely over after Culloden (1746), Scotland was at peace and the house did not need to be fortified as it would have been in the past. The title of Earl was raised to Marquess (1790) and finally to Duke of Abercorn (1868). The coat of arms is very similar to that of the related family of the Dukes of Hamilton. Both contain five-pointed stars (for Hamilton), ships with oars in action (for Arran) and three fleur-de-lys (for Châtellerault), a French Dukedom that the family also claims.

In 1760 the 8th Earl commissioned the house from Sir William Chambers (1723-1796), who had also created Somerset House in London. It is Chambers' only classical country house to have survived unaltered, and his only country house in Scotland.

The brief was 'to build a modest but elegant house suitable for a confirmed bachelor'. Hamilton lived mostly in Cavendish Square, London and installed a site manager to supervise the work. His occasional visits while the house was under construction seem to have provoked extensive debate.

Building started in 1763 and was completed in 1769: progress was much hampered by severe winter weather and the disagreements between Hamilton and his architect. The house has a strictly symmetrical frontage and a splendid Corinthian portico. Together with its adjacent courtyard, it forms the finest Palladian ensemble in the Edinburgh area. It was considered one of the most elegant private residences in Edinburgh when it was built. It is Grade-A listed and celebrated its 250th anniversary in 2019.

Corinthian columns

Creature comforts were well catered for at Duddingston House. It had an ice house which is Grade-C listed. You can still see this on the edge of the golf course on the north side of Cavalry Park Drive. The idea of ice houses came from Italy in the 1660s and soon every rich family had one. The structure was sunk into the ground, with further insulation provided by sawdust. Ice blocks came by sea from as far as Norway. The Earl and his guests could have enjoyed cold drinks and cold desserts, perhaps with a hint of sawdust – unless the ship was becalmed, when it would arrive without any ice, just a cargo of tepid water.

The Earl was said to be very well mannered and on close terms with King George III. It was a rule of the royal court that no one should ever contradict His Majesty. One day George III rode out from Windsor with a large party and decided to call in for breakfast with the Earl at his London residence, giving little notice. The King said afterwards, 'Ha, Lord Abercorn, I fear that we put you to a great deal of trouble the other morning'. Not wishing to contradict the King, Abercorn replied 'A great deal of trouble, may it please Your Majesty'. The King and bystanders were apparently much amused.

Abercorn never married but retained a vast number of servants. The household needed five carriages to travel around the country, and he often commuted between Duddingston and London, in those days a protracted and arduous undertaking. It was on one such journey from London in 1789 that he died, and the estate then passed to his nephew who became the 9th Earl.

Entrance hall ceiling

The total cost of building Duddingston House and its pleasure grounds was over £30,000 (at least £6 million in today's money). It was designed for lavish entertaining, rather than for long-term occupation. A huge part of the interior is taken up by a grand entrance hall with a sweeping staircase, occupying over one-third of the total volume of the house. Design was a constant source of tension between the 8th Earl and his architect. Dissatisfied with what he perceived as a lack of grandeur, the Earl instructed Chambers to move the staircase further back despite the advanced stage of construction. The legacy of this conflict is visible in the intrusion of the top of the staircase into the decorative cornice.

In about 1800, Duddingston House was rented from the Abercorn estate by the Earl of Moira, a veteran of the American War of Independence (1775-83) and

The Earl of Moira

Bannister detail

commander of the army in Scotland. His wife Flora puzzled Edinburgh society by sending out cards which read simply 'The Countess of Loudon and Moira At Home'. This was a new, informal style which baffled the recipients. Was it an invitation?

However, the couple became very popular in Edinburgh for their fine hospitality. At one party at the house on 14 June 1805 they gave a Grand Fete receiving three hundred of the nobility, naval and military gentlemen, judges and gentry from the city. The house was 'brilliantly fitted up with festoons and flowers and embellished with a naval pillar with the names of Nelson, Howe and other admirals'.

In the 20th century the property stood vacant for many years and was in poor condition. It was bought in 1960 by Edward Gladstone who restored it thoroughly and opened it as the Mansion House Hotel in 1963. The hotel operated for some years, but sadly it had

The main staircase

too few rooms to be economically viable. After planning permission to add bedrooms was declined, the hotel had to close.

After that, the house's internal condition declined further. The courtyard buildings had become derelict and were restored only in the 1990s, when new houses were also begun nearby (architect Simister Monaghan). The present owner is architect Bruce Hare, who joined the Percy Johnson-Marshall Partnership in 1985 when the principal retired. Percy Johnson-Marshall (1915-93) was a long-term resident of Bella Vista in the village. As a modernist architect, he was well known for extensive developments carried out by Edinburgh University in the 1960s.

Duddingston House Properties completed the last major refurbishment in 1990 and the house now functions as offices for it and its tenants.

The driveway and parking areas are private, so please do not bring in vehicles unless invited. However you are welcome to walk into the grounds from the gates at Milton Road West or Cavalry Park Drive. The two approaches are linked by a clearly signed pedestrian Right of Way.

41 Courtyard

Beside the house and joined to it only by a small corridor is a U-Shaped courtyard in the same architectural style. On the south side were the servants' quarters and the kitchens, whilst on the north side were the stables. Although they needed very large doors at the rear for the carriages, the courtyard is cleverly designed so that both sides of the courtyard look identical, giving it a pleasing symmetry.

As a result, the kitchens were quite distant from the main house and the food would likely have become cold while in transit along the corridor. However, at least if the kitchen caught fire (a common occurrence in those days) the main house was less likely to burn down. Joining the two arms is a colonnade and what may have been the house of the estate factor, the laundry and a clock tower with no clock.

The main house and adjacent courtyard fell into disrepair before and after World War 2, and were used at that time by the army. The Courtyard was restored in the 1990s and converted into private houses.

The clock tower

Looking west, Arthur's Seat provides a dramatic backdrop to the view from Duddingston House and its gardens, now the golf course. The house, courtyard and gardens are private, but you can see them clearly from the driveway.

West over the courtyard

42 The pleasure gardens

The direct approach to Duddingston House from the village is by a single-track road called Cavalry Park Drive which approaches the backs of the buildings. However, the main entrance is at the bend in Milton Road West through the Grade-B listed gates with curved screen walls. The drive leads up through the golf course to an impressive view of the main house with courtyard to its right. Before reaching the private access to these buildings, the Right of Way continues on a path to the right.

The lands of Duddingston were purchased by the 8th Earl of Abercorn in 1745 from the Duke of Argyll. Only 15 years later, the Earl commissioned a design for a splendid Palladian mansion mainly for hosting entertainment: see pages 78-81. In the 1760s the estate was laid out as pleasure gardens by James Robertson in the style of Capability Brown, with shrubberies, canals, lakes, cascades, grottos, statues and a folly or 'temple'.

The grounds covered a huge area (200 acres) and involved the demolition of five acres of the village, reducing its population from about 500 to about 200. The gardens covered not only the present site of the golf club but also extended to the west, to an area now used as recreational playing fields, operated by Edinburgh Council and much valued by the community.

Within the fields, there is a mound with magnificent mature trees that probably date to the 8th Earl of Abercorn's era.

When Lord Moira lived there, he held various mock battles and sieges in and around the pleasure gardens and around Duddingston and Craigmillar with nearly 10,000 'fencibles and volunteers'. He devised a succession of manoeuvres which presented a vivid image of the art of war. *Fencibles* (from the word defencible) were British Army regiments raised in the United Kingdom and in the colonies for defence against the threat of invasion during the Seven Years' War, the American War of Independence and French Revolutionary Wars in the late 18th century.

Sir Walter Scott knew Lord Moira well, but was unkind about him. He *'regretted the foibles which mingled with his character, so as to make his noble qualities sometimes questionable, sometimes ridiculous. He had a high reputation for war, but it was after the pettifogging hostilities in America where he had done clever things ... He had an overmastering degree of vanity of the grossest kind… like a ring in his nose, into which any rogue might put a string.'*

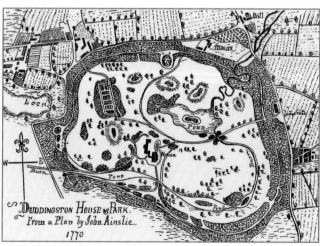

DUDDINGSTON HOUSE & PARK.
From a Plan by John Ainslie.
1770

The temple

The pleasure gardens later fell into disrepair and were converted into a golf course. Screened by the trees stands the 'temple' or folly that is the only remnant of Lord Abercorn's pleasure gardens. Designed by Chambers in 1768, this elegant building is Grade-A listed. The dome was restored by pupils from Holy Rood High School in 1973.

 As the temple stands on a private golf course, it cannot be safely or responsibly approached at any time when golf is, or might be, in play.

The driveway crosses a bridge over the Braid Burn which passes through the estate on its way to the sea at Portobello. It originates in the Pentland Hills and is about nine miles long; it name changes to Figgate Burn near Duddingston crossroads. While walking through the grounds keep an eye out for roe deer, and look on the left for the outline of Craigmillar Castle on the skyline.

Above: The 'temple'
Below: The 13th green

44 Duddingston Golf Club

In 1894-5 the financial community of Edinburgh created a golf course on the former parkland around Duddingston House. It was designed by Willie Park, three times winner of the Open. Later extensions in the 1960s and 70s brought the course length up to 6525 yards (nearly 6 km). Until 1919, the club was known as the Insurance and Banking Golf Club.

The course was laid out on part of the deer parkland in the estate of the Earls of Abercorn. This was developed at the time when the 8th Earl built Duddingston House. The Roman Doric 'temple' to the right of the 13th green appears (simplified) in the club's logo.

The Braid burn creates much interest in playing the course as it crosses several fairways, making a trap for the unwary. In former times this burn supplied the power for Duddingston Mills. Part of the course covered the area where Bonnie Prince Charlie's cavalry had camped in 1745 prior to their victory at the Battle of Prestonpans: see page 57. Their presence is commemorated in the names of the Cavalry Park playing fields and Cavalry Park Drive which follows the western edge of the golf course down to the modern housing development.

The club has its own war memorial which was unveiled in June 1921. The deceased include 37 of the 176 club members who had served during World War 1. The course enjoys an excellent reputation and regularly hosts amateur open events.

The clubhouse is reached from Duddingston Road West and its restaurant is open to the general public. It serves food and drink during the day, and also snacks on summer evenings.

45 War memorials

After the end of the Great War in 1918, almost every community in Britain erected a memorial to local people who had died. In Duddingston this proved to be a controversial issue. The Kirk's plan for a memorial built into the church wall was opposed by those in the community who wanted a village monument separate from the church. In the event, two separate memorials were created, and on every Remembrance Sunday wreathes are still laid at both.

The village memorial is opposite the eastern end of Old Church Lane on Duddingston Road West. It is a free-standing Celtic wheel cross, 18 ft (5·5 m) tall, with decorative relief carvings on its upper parts. The memorial is one of eight designed by George Washington Browne, a well-known Edinburgh architect who lost three sons in the Great War. Browne contributed greatly to Edinburgh's architecture; the Caledonian (now Waldorf-Astoria) Hotel, Sick Kids' Hospital and Central Library are among his works.

In October 1921 the memorial was unveiled by the Duke of Abercorn who had donated the small piece of land on which it stands. The main costs, however, were met by public subscription. Unfortunately, it was blown down in a severe gale the following year. When it was re-erected, iron supports were attached to the rear to prevent any recurrence: they are still in place.

The church's memorial is a wall tablet to the right of the new entrance into the building. It was unveiled in 1922 by Edinburgh's Lord Provost Hutchison. The tablet lists the names of 29 men of the parish who had died in the conflict – almost a quarter of the 130 local men

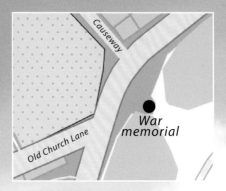

who had served in the forces. The list includes a son of the Duke of Abercorn and the three Hay brothers who are also commemorated inside the Kirk: see pages 22 and 28.

Celtic wheel cross at top of memorial

46 Lady Nairne's Lodge

The Premier Inn that stands near Duddingston crossroads has historic interest that belies its status as a budget hotel. The clues are in the name of its restaurant, the Lady Nairne, and the age of its building, formerly called Carolina Cottage, then Nairne Lodge. 'Lady Nairne' also features in many street names nearby, but who was she?

Lady Carolina Nairne (1766-1845) was a poet and a prolific collector and writer of ballads and songs. She was an early admirer of Robert Burns, and indeed her work was rated by many as second only to his. Born as Carolina Oliphant in Gask House, Strathearn, she and her parents were strongly Jacobite. Her father Laurence Oliphant had gone into exile after Culloden and his lands were confiscated. Later the property was purchased and restored by relatives.

Above: Lady Carolina Nairne
Lady Nairne's Lodge

She wrote many famous Scottish ballads, some lyrical celebrations of countryside such as The Rowan Tree and Jacobite anthems, including *Charlie is my darling, The hundred pipers* and *Will ye no come back again*. Few have ever heard of her, because she cultivated obscurity during her lifetime, using the pseudonym B.B. (Mrs Bogan of Bogan).

In 1806 she married her second cousin, Major William Murray Nairne, and they moved to Portobello. Later they moved to Duddingston, where they remained until his death in 1830. She kept her writing secret from him, fearing that it would affect her position in society. Her work appeared (under B.B.) in a collection *The Scottish Minstrel* published between 1821 and 1824, but she even tried to disguise herself from its editor whom she visited in a hooded cloak. Not until after her death was her work properly attributed. Her sister published a collection of 87 of Carolina's verse and songs under the title *Lays from Strathearn* (1846).

47 Cauvin's Hospital

On the north-west corner of Duddingston crossroads stands a large building that now forms the heart of Willowbrae Sheltered Housing Complex. It is a Grade-B two-storey classical villa which was originally built in about 1806 as a private house for Louis Cauvin (1754-1825), who named it Louisfield. Cauvin was a wealthy teacher of French, his most famous pupil being Robert Burns who in 1787 had lessons three nights a week. He commended the poet, who 'learned more in three months than most people did in three years'.

Three Friends

Cauvin habitually rose at 4 am and often worked a 14-hour day, combining teaching with farming and property dealing. He was an astute businessman, and did not like to be bested in a dispute. When he built a tower (known locally as Cauvin's Folly) on his rising ground behind the Causeway, his neighbour Colonel Graham, then owner of Bella Vista, objected to being overlooked and raised his boundary wall. Cauvin promptly had his tower made higher, and this escalation was repeated.

By the time Cauvin died he had amassed £30,000, then a large fortune, and bequeathed it all in a philanthropic will. After his death in 1825 the house was enlarged as a 'hospital' for the education of 20 sons of teachers, farmers, master printers, booksellers and 'respectable' agricultural workers. 'Cauvin's Hospital' opened in 1833 and the boys received six years of education including Latin, Greek, French, German, mathematics, physics, chemistry and botany.

In John Kay's etching of Three Friends (1817), Cauvin is the central character. To the left is Robert Kay, an architect who designed elevations for South Bridge and built a house for himself at 30 the Causeway (Sycamore Bank) in 1810. On the right is David Scott who farmed at Northfield, and was an elder at Duddingston Kirk.

Cauvin was also an elder at Duddingston Kirk, and he disliked long sermons. His seat was at the front of the gallery, easily seen by his friend the minister, John Thomson: see page 12. When Cauvin felt that the sermon had tried his patience, he used to signal this by swinging his large gold watch by its chain; the good-natured minister apparently often took the hint.

Former Cauvin's Hospital

48 Duddingston crossroads

Mayfield, 126 Duddingston Road

Most people arriving by bus will alight at Duddingston crossroads, a busy junction with lots of interest. Dominating the crossroads at its north corner is a handsome Grade-B listed house, its address 126 Duddingston Road. Formerly known as Mayfield, it was built after Duddingston Estate had the road widened by demolishing a row of cottages in 1914.

Mayfield has a fine conical entrance turret, crow-stepped gables and 12-pane glazing, along with other apparently 17th century Scottish features. In fact it was built in 1914 to a design by architects Leadbetter, Fairley and Reid. The interior of the house was extensively modernised in the 1950s, but its exterior is largely original.

The same architects designed the interesting Grade-C listed development at 31-33 Duddingston Mills, slightly further north. This includes an unusual small tenement consisting of just three flats on two storeys. It appears much older than the early 19th century cottages opposite, but small art nouveau touches give away its true date. Next to it stands Duddingston Forge, a single-storey U-shaped building with an attic. It is Grade-B listed and continues to work as a smithy and forge, specialising in decorative ironwork.

The crossroads has further interest, with Objects 46 and 47 on its west side: see pages 87 and 88. On its south corner, look for a blue police box embedded in a garden wall. Most British cities had police boxes to allow officers to talk to their police stations, report incidents and receive instructions. Most boxes resembled the London model, made famous as Doctor Who's Tardis. However, Edinburgh's were unique: their more classical design was by City Architect Ebenezer MacRae. Of the original 142, at least half remain around the city – some used as coffee stalls or information points, others derelict.

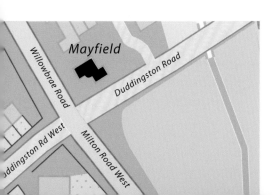

49 Prestonfield House

Prestonfield House stands on the opposite side of Duddingston Loch from the village. The main building was designed in 1687 by the king's architect Sir William Bruce, and is Grade-A listed. It has been extended several times, mainly in the 19th century. Nearby stands the spectacular stable block designed as a rotunda by James Gillespie Graham in 1816, another Grade-A listed building.

Main house from the west

The complex was designed as a country manor house, but now functions as a hotel. The estate was originally known as Priestfield, but after the Reformation the name was thought too Catholic-sounding and was changed to Prestonfield. However the nearby church on Dalkeith Road, albeit Protestant, is still called Priestfield.

The estate has had a colourful history. After 1630 it became closely, if scandalously, linked to Duddingston Kirk when Robert Menteith (1603-60) became the minister. He was then a friend and ally of Sir James Hamilton, Prestonfield's owner. Together they arranged for the whole estate to be added to Duddingston Parish – a decision that required the Kirk to be enlarged by the addition of the Prestonfield Aisle.

Menteith's ministry, and his friendship with Hamilton, were both short-lived. He had an affair with Hamilton's wife, Anna Hepburn. Menteith used to row across the loch to spend the night with her when her husband was away. Their 'illicit amour' was reported to the Privy Council in 1633, causing him to flee to France, where he became a Catholic and a protegé of Cardinal Richelieu.

Stable block

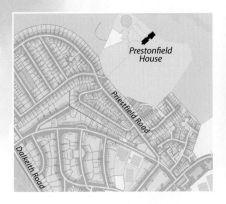

By 1677, the estate had been crippled by debt and was sold to the Dick family, two of whose members served as Lord Provost of Edinburgh. The second, Sir James Dick, undertook at his own expense to clear the filthy streets of the Old Town of human and animal excrement, using the stinking 'night soil' to fertilise the ground of his estate.

A later family member, Sir Alexander Dick, helped to found the Royal Society of Edinburgh. His success in introducing rhubarb to Scotland is celebrated in the name of the hotel's gourmet restaurant. For details, see page 93.

Over the years, Prestonfield's interior has been enhanced with lavish furnishings from all over Europe and paintings ranging from Italian-style landscape frescos to formal portraits. During the Enlightenment, Sir Alexander played generous host to such visitors as David Hume, Benjamin Franklin, Dr Johnson and his biographer James Boswell. More recently the hotel has welcomed prime ministers Winston Churchill and Margaret Thatcher, and stars such as Sean Connery, Elton John and Catherine Zeta Jones.

Above: Plaster phoenix on ceiling
Below: Marble Hall with staircase

50 The Innocent railway

The Innocent railway is the oldest in the Edinburgh area, and indeed one of the oldest in the UK. The concept was born in the 1820s when a group of coal mine owners in Dalkeith wanted to transport their coal cheaply to Edinburgh. The growing city was consuming a rapidly increasing amount of coal, but the poor condition of local roads meant that it had to be brought in by sea from Fife and as far away as Northumberland. The railway opened in stages from 1831.

Although intended purely as a goods line with a track gauge of 4 ft 6, a local businessman started operating a passenger service in 1832. Originally the trains were pulled by horses, and by steam engines only after 1845. This was when the company was absorbed into the North British Railway, its gauge standardised and the track strengthened. Passenger traffic ceased in 1860 but goods were carried until 1968.

The origin of the name 'innocent' is debatable. The plaque near the beginning of the line suggests that horse-drawn rail travel was seen as pastoral compared with steam. However, contemporary sources suggest that it

Freight train on the Innocent in the 1950s

reflects its innocence of any deaths among its construction workers – an unusual achievement for that era.

This safety record is all the more impressive given that the line includes a long tunnel – the first on any public railway in Britain and 1700 ft long. The final approach to the terminus at St Leonard's was too steep for the horses (at 1 in 30), so a stationary steam engine hauled the wagons up the rope-worked incline.

After the railway closed, the trackbed between St Leonard's and Brunstane became a cycleway. Visitors can still walk through the tunnel, follow the cycleway through the park and visit the cast iron bridge at Forkenford – Grade-B listed and one of the earliest of its type (1831). The Innocent runs along the southern extreme of Duddingston's Conservation Area, and it is the last of our 50 Objects.

Useful bus services

Reaching Duddingston from central Edinburgh is easy. Frequent buses (14 per hour on weekdays) serve Duddingston Crossroads via Willowbrae Road, with some faster buses (X5, X7 and X44) stopping short at Paisley Drive. From the Crossroads to the village is half a mile (800 m).

The alternative is the number 42 which goes to the village, but its route is indirect so it takes longer from the city centre, and is less frequent (normally half hourly but only hourly on Sundays).

Holyrood Park

No buses run through Holyrood Park, and every Sunday the road is closed to vehicles from 8.30 am, making it pleasanter for walkers and cyclists. Reopening times vary with the season: see website for Object 17 on page 95 for details.

(Map labels: Paisley Drive; X5, X7, X44; A1 Willowbrae Road; from city; 4, 44, 104, 113; Duddingston Crossroads; Duddingston Road West; 42; to city; Duddingston Village; 42; Old Church Lane; from city; Duddingston Golf Course)

Eating and drinking

Bizzy Lizzy
98 Duddingston Road West, EH15 3PU
Open weekdays in school termtime only, from 6.30 to 14.30 Mondays-Thursdays but closes 13.30 on Fridays

Garden Room
Millar Hall, 15 Old Church Lane, EH15 3PX
Staffed by volunteers, so hours vary. In 2019 closed Mondays and Tuesdays, with variable hours on Wednesdays through to Sundays. In 2019, open March to October only.

Duddingston Golf Club
Duddingston Road West, EH15 3QD
Meals year-round in the daytime, also snacks on summer evenings. Times vary: phone 0131 661 7688.

Lady Nairne (Beefeater)
Premier Inn
228 Willowbrae Road, EH8 7NG
Food served daily year-round 12.00 to 22.00.

Prestonfield House
Priestfield Road, EH16 5UT
Open year-round for bar lunches and fine dining: see website (page 95) for hours and reservations.

Sheep Heid Inn
43-45 The Causeway, EH15 3QA
Open daily year-round 12.00 to 23.00 (24.00 at weekends), food normally served up to 21.00.

Duddingston Conservation Society

This book was sponsored by the Society which was established in 1959 and welcomes new members who live within Duddingston Conservation Area: see page 5. It also welcomes hearing from those who live outside the area but support its goals.

For details, please see its website: *www.duddingstonvillageconservationsociety.wordpress.com* where you can also download copies of the DCS newsletter, *The Paddock*.

Glossary

art nouveau   style of decorative art/architecture that was most popular between about 1890 and 1914 in Europe

ashlar   dressed stone of regular shape and smooth surface

astragal   divisions between panes of glass within a window

bairn (Scots)   child

beadle   church officer responsible for preparing premises for worship and other duties

Bronze Age   in Britain, prehistoric period from c. 2500 BC to c. 700 BC when people made tools from copper and bronze

burn (Scots)   stream

cornice   decorative feature that crowns a wall or building; on roofs, a cornice sometimes projects in order to shed rainwater

crow-stepped   decorative steps used to finish a roof gable tidily

curling   sport in which players slide granite stones across ice, aiming at a target area; demands strategy and accuracy

elder   ordained office-holder elected by a Presbyterian congregation

Enlightenment   in Scotland, a period between about 1730-1820 when great thinkers made major contributions to the arts and sciences

feu   a plot of land under the feudal system of land tenure which subsisted in Scotland until its abolition in 2000

folly   garden structure built for a decorative purpose, with no useful function

gable   where two roof pitches meet, the section of wall (often triangular) is known as a gable

glebe (Scots)   land provided to a minister, originally for grazing his horse, later usually let for cultivation

gowl (Scots)   deep hollow between hills: hence Windy Gowl in Holyrood Park

Hardings   coarse cloth woven from reeds to make sacking

harl (Scots)   protective rough finish to a wall consisting of lime with small pebbles thrown on using a special trowel

Jacobite   see text opposite

Kirk Session   governing body of a church, composed of its minister and elders with responsibility for spiritual and temporal affairs

Listed Buildings   system of classifying buildings and other objects according to their heritage value: in Scotland the grades are A to C

manse (Scots)   house tied to the Kirk and occupied by the minister

pediment   decorative feature, often triangular, placed above doors and windows of classical buildings to adorn them

Presbytery   governing body of an area to which many churches belong, e.g. Edinburgh

Reformation   movement in 16th century Europe to challenge Roman Catholic doctrine and papal authority; it led to Protestantism

Resurrectionists   grave robbers who stole and sold freshly buried corpses

rig and furrow   a method of cultivation that creates ridges and furrows

Royal Society of Edinburgh   established in 1783, this body is effectively the national academy of Scotland

rubble   rough stone of irregular shape and rough surface

tenement   multi-occupancy building with main doors typically opening from a shared staircase

Who were the Jacobites?

In 1688, King James VII of Scotland (who was also James II of England) was deposed by popular demand and fled the country. He was a Catholic and, after his wife gave birth to a son, people feared a continuing Catholic succession. His Protestant daughter Mary was installed in his place, along with her Dutch husband William of Orange, also a Protestant. Over much of the 18th century, the Jacobites (supporters of James or *Jacobus*) tried to restore James VII and his heirs to the throne. The last and most serious of these attempts was the rising of 1745, led by the grandson of James VII – Charles Edward Stuart or 'Bonnie Prince Charlie'.

Encouraged by their success at the Battle of Prestonpans (see page 57), the Jacobites marched on into England where they received little support. At Derby they turned back and were forced to retreat all the way to northern Scotland. Britain's last civil war ended on 16 April 1746 at Culloden Moor, near Inverness. Culloden was the last battle fought on British soil, and was a decisive defeat for the Jacobites, whose losses of 1500-2000 far outnumbered government caualties of about 300 redcoats. The Prince escaped 'over the sea to Skye' to live out the rest of his life in Italy. The Jacobite cause has been much romanticised and extensively celebrated in songs by Robert Burns and Lady Nairne among others: see page 87.

Further reading

We refer to two booklets, both sold by the Garden Room at the Kirk and perhaps unavailable otherwise. The first is undated, but clearly precedes the Parry booklet of 2009. There is extensive overlap between the two.

Cruickshank, William G *Duddingston Kirk and Village* 32pp

Parry, Agnes (rev 2009) *Duddingston Kirk Through the Ages* 72 pp

We consulted too many books to list here. Four of the most useful are:

Baird, William (1898) *Annals of Duddingston and Portobello* Andrew Elliot (facsimile edition from Forgotten Books 978-0-282-64090-3)

Baird, William (2nd ed, 1907) *John Thomson of Duddingston, Pastor and Painter* Oliphant, Anderson and Ferrier (facsimile edition from Forgotten Books 978-0-259-78856-0)

Ferguson, Sir James (1972) *Balloon Tytler* Faber and Faber 0-571-09986-6

White, Dennis B (1990) *Old Duddingston and Portobello* Mainstream 1-85158-299-1.

Useful websites

For information on Listed buildings, we recommend the Historic Environment Scotland website, especially using their map search feature:

www.historicenvironment.scot.

We also made great use of SCRAN (*www.scran.ac.uk*) and Canmore (*www.canmore.org.uk*). The table below shows websites that relate to specific objects in the book.

Object	pages	website
1	15	*www.duddingstonkirk.co.uk*
10	34	*www.drneilsgarden.co.uk*
14	40-42	*scottishwildlifetrust.org.uk/reserve/bawsinch-and-duddingston*
17	44-47	*www.historicenvironment.scot/visit-a-place/places/holyrood-park*
20,21	49,50	*www.nms.ac.uk/national-museum-of-scotland*
23	52	*www.thesheepheidedinburgh.co.uk*
28	61	*www.chalkworks.com*
36-39	72-77	*duddingstonvillageconservationsociety.wordpress.com*
40-42	78-83	*www.duddingstonhouse.co.uk*
43-44	84-85	*www.duddingstongolfclub.co.uk*
49	90-91	*www.prestonfield.com*

Disclaimer

We tried to check facts and dates, but information was often conflicting. We consulted many sources, printed and online, and visited various archives – those of the Society, the Kirk and the Trotters, and the National Archive of Scotland. Inevitably there will be readers who know more: please email us: *jacquetta@rucsacs.com*. We will share all such updates and amendments on our web page *www.rucsacs.com/books/dcs.*

Thanks & credits

The Society warmly thanks all those who contributed text: the hard graft of writing was a team effort by Keir Bloomer, Roger Crofts, Leo Harding, Jim Jack, Nick Marshall, Jacquetta Megarry, Susan Mercer and Malcolm Windsor. Each author drafted between 1 and 15 Objects, and collaborated over editing.

The Society thanks also those who offered information, loaned equipment and were helpful over access: this includes all of the above and also Sarah Boyack, Tony Cavar, Tim and Sarah Chalk, Tracey Robinson, Emma and Tom Fitzgerald, Carn Gibson, Jill and James Gilchrist, Basti Geller, Alasdair Gill, Ted Gladstone, Martin Goldie, Bruce Hare, Christian and Dot Henson, Richard Inglis, Pauline McQuade, Mary Moultrie, Freda O'Byrne, Kay and Robin Orr, David Purdie, Iain and Morag Torrance, Kenny Train, Gaynor and Steve Turner, Kathleen White.

We warmly thank **Madeleine MacKenzie** for her painstaking work in proofreading the entire book so carefully.

Photo credits & invitation

We thank the following for permission to reproduce their images. We tried to trace the rights owner of every photo. If a reader knows the original source of any uncredited image, please email us (*jacquetta@rucsacs.com*) so we can credit it fully on our web page *www.rucsacs.com/books/dcs.* Sandy Bloomer 56u; Ian Clydesdale 53l, title page and 54 (inset sign), 49; Louise Cooper 47u, 48 (both); Roger Crofts 10-11, 40u, 40-1, 42-3, 44u, 45u, 46u; Dreamstime.com and 3 photographers Егор Балясов 4-5, Ccx1010 8-9, Joan Egert 41u; Duddingston Golf Club 84-5; Christian Henson 6-7, 64-5, 70, 74-5, back cover flap; Historic Environment Scotland 71u; William Hole 9; John Kay 88; Mapio.net 16; Graham McGirk 34u; Susan Mercer 24, 37; Freda O'Byrne 72, 73 (both), 77 (both); Frank Parry front cover (main); Prestonfield House 90 (both), 91 (both); Ildiko Rusvai @edienthusiast front cover foreground; Sheep Heid 55l; Hamish Stevenson Collection 92 (both); Kenny Train 23; Trotters Club archive 55u; Unsplash Yves Alarie 44-5; Wikimedia Commons 8, 12, 42 (Krzysztof Ziarnek).

We reproduce ten historic photos, postcards and engravings for which we cannot trace sources. Excluding all those above, the 99 remaining photos including back cover and insets are © **Jacquetta Megarry 2019**.

Index

A

Abbey Laird 45, 67
Abercorn, 8th Earl of 10, 58, 62, 71, 78-80, 83
Arthur's Seat 6, 8, 44, 46-7, 50, 51, 61, 82

B

Bawsinch Nature Reserve 8, 42
Bonnie Prince Charlie 10, 53, 57, 68, 83, 85, 94
Bronze Age 4, 8, 44, 45, 49
Burke and Hare 50
Burns, Robert 67, 87, 88, 94
bus information 93
byre 73, 76

C

Causeway, the 9, 11, 43, 53, 61, 64-7, 68-71, 76, 88
Cauvin, Louis 88
Chambers, William 78, 80, 84
community garden 72, 77
Community Land Group 11, 72-3, 74
curling 10, 38-9, 50

D

Disruption 19, 29
Dr Neils Garden 34-5, 36-9
Duddingston Conservation Society 4, 11, 93, 95
Duddingston Golf Club 85, 93
Duddingston Hardings 43
Duddingston Hoard 9, 49
Duddingston House & Courtyard 6, 10, 11, 78-81, 82, 83
Duddingston Kirk 6, 8, 9, 15-9, 20-8, 24, 26, 58, 86, 88, 90
Duddingston Loch 6, 38-9, 40-1, 42, 49, 56
Duddingston village 4, 6, 8, 9, 10, 11, 43, 46, 58-77, 83

E

Enlightenment, Scottish 10-11, 13, 56, 93

F

field and orchard 74-5
food and drink 93

G

Gatehouse 24-5
glebe 33
graveyard and entrance 26, 27-9
grave robbers 11, 24, 27

H

Hamilton, James 10, 58, 62, 71, 78-80, 83
Hay brothers 11, 22, 28, 86
Holyrood Park 4, 44-5, 51, 93
Hutton, James 8, 13, 47

I

Innocent railway 42, 92

J

Jacobites 10, 57, 78, 83, 87, 94

M

manse 13, 30-31, 59
Menteith, Robert 90
Millar Hall 32
miniature coffins 50

N

Nairne, Lady Carolina 87
National Museum of Scotland 9, 49, 50, 95

O

Old Church Lane 9, 11, 58-60, 63, 64, 72

P

Pinkerton 22
pleasure gardens and 'temple' 83-4
Prestonfield Aisle 17, 19, 20, 22, 90
Prestonfield House 90-1, 93
Prestonpans, Battle of 10, 57, 68, 82, 87, 94

Q

Queen Margaret 8, 9
Queen Victoria & Prince Albert 11, 45, 48

R

Raeburn, Henry 12, 13, 56
reedbeds 42, 43
Reformation 9, 10, 16, 17
Resurrectionists 24
Royal Society of Edinburgh 10, 13, 93

S

Scott, Walter 11, 12, 13, 31, 49, 53, 61, 83
Sheep Heid 6, 9, 11, 26, 52-3, 54-7, 71, 93
skating 10, 38-9, 56, 57, 59
skittles 55
snuff box 4, 54

T

Thomson, John 10, 11, 12-14, 19, 22, 29, 30, 31, 41, 61, 62, 88, 95
Thomson Tower 13, 38-9
Turner, J M W 11, 13, 38-9
Tytler, James 67, 95

W

war memorials 11, 86, 87
Waterloo walnut 31